The
PESCATARIAN
COOKBOOK

Baked Salmon with Greek Veggies & Avocado Tzatziki, page 118

The
PESCATARIAN
COOKBOOK

THE ESSENTIAL KITCHEN COMPANION

Cara Harbstreet, MS, RD, LD

Photography by Darren Muir

ROCKRIDGE PRESS

Dedicated to my husband, whose tireless support and endless patience make endeavors like this possible.

CONTENTS

INTRODUCTION

*F*ood has a way of stirring up some of our best memories. Many of my favorites include my father. When I taste smoked trout, I think of a fishing-permit mishap from one of his trips to Arkansas. After going over the limit—and paying the fine—our freezer was stocked with trout for months, and that solidified my palate for the smoked version. Not only that, but it helped me develop an understanding and appreciation of the seafood on my plate and a connection to nature and family—and we still tease my mom for her distaste for anything with fins still attached. Tuna steaks make me think of the fish my father caught and shipped on dry ice in a cooler. And my first experience with raw oysters took place on our family farm in rural Missouri, about as far from any coast as you can get. But my dad decided we were going to have oysters, and we're a stubborn family by nature, so he made it happen.

Although I credit him with introducing me to many of my favorite meals, there were other influences along the way that helped shape my transition to a plant-forward, pescatarian style of eating. I didn't always have a balanced or healthy relationship with food. As I learned to practice intuitive eating and heal my relationship with food, I found that I kept gravitating back to this style of food. With a plant-forward, pescatarian diet, there's so much variety that I've yet to get bored with using my same favorite ingredients. In this cookbook, I will show you many ways to get creative in the kitchen.

Despite my lifelong love of seafood, I've always lived in a landlocked area. That's the reality for the vast majority of readers of this book. Because it's challenging at times to source seafood that I feel confident eating, I took it upon myself to learn more about the sustainability issues surrounding seafood. I was able to teach myself and my clients how to make the most of the ingredients that we have readily available. I can't wait to share my knowledge with you because I know that most Americans fall short of the recommendation of two servings of seafood per week. Introducing fish and seafood into familiar, comforting, satisfying recipes can be one of many ways to improve the overall quality of your diet, all while embracing mindful eating techniques and viewing nutrition as a way to live out your values.

In writing this book, I wanted to create a resource to help people like me: those who want to reap the benefits of a pescatarian diet without breaking the bank. I also wanted to showcase how familiar ingredients can be transformed into unique and interesting dishes inspired by global cuisines. I try my best to bring that influence into my own kitchen through aromatic herbs, seasonings, and sauces from beyond my region.

The recipes you'll see in this book include some of my most tried-and-true favorites. Pistachio-Crusted Shrimp & Grits (page 107), Seafood Gumbo-Laya (page 76)—a semi-blasphemous take on two classic Cajun dishes—and Salmon Burgers with Crunchy Cabbage Slaw (page 103) are versions of dishes that I grew up eating, and they spark the nostalgia of many early food memories. Those were days long before I learned all about food during my educational journey to become a registered dietitian. Today, in my work with intuitive eating and a non-diet approach, I help people rediscover joy in eating meals like these. Food is meant to nourish our bodies, but it can do so much more. If nothing else, I hope these recipes inspire you to try something different or find a new way to connect with your food.

Cheers to creating fearlessly nourishing meals!

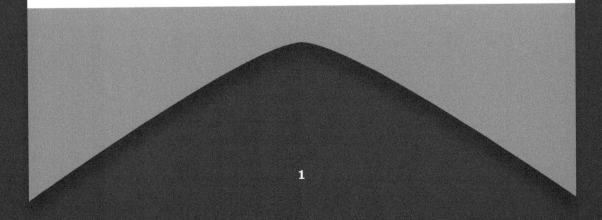

THE PESCATARIAN DIET AND YOUR HEALTH

THE PESCATARIAN DIET

To get started on our pescatarian diet journey, we need to learn more about it. *Pesce* is Italian for "fish." A pescatarian diet is similar to a Mediterranean diet, or to a vegetarian diet with the addition of fish and seafood. This eating style emphasizes minimally processed ingredients and whole-food sources for carbohydrates, protein, and fat. Here are some of the other defining features of this style of eating:

THE 5 MAJOR PRINCIPLES OF THE PESCATARIAN DIET

If you're new to a pescatarian lifestyle, there are several key components to remember. Although there is much variety and flexibility in this style of eating, some of the most common features are listed below.

1. **Fish and Seafood as Primary Animal Proteins:** A pescatarian diet includes fresh and saltwater fish, shellfish, and crustaceans. You won't see ingredients such as beef, pork, poultry, wild game, or other meats in this book.

2. **The Ability to Include Eggs and Dairy:** Many pescatarians choose to include eggs and dairy as protein sources. However, there are some who prefer to rely solely on fish and seafood for animal protein. The best part about the pescatarian diet is that the choice is up to you.

3. **Plant-Forward Focus:** Many people gravitate toward plant-based eating for health or environmental concerns. A pescatarian diet is similar in that regard and can offer a realistic compromise for people who don't want to go fully vegetarian.

4. **Lots of Fruits and Vegetables:** A pescatarian diet encourages high intake of fruits and vegetables. These are nutrient-rich ingredients that

provide many essential vitamins and minerals, as well as beneficial antioxidants and phytochemicals for health.

5. **Whole Grains and Fiber-Rich Foods:** A pescatarian diet is not meant to be a low-carbohydrate diet. It includes carbohydrates from whole grains and other starchy or fiber-rich foods such as potatoes, legumes, and ancient grains.

10 COMMON QUESTIONS ABOUT A PESCATARIAN DIET

It's not unusual to have questions or concerns about adding more fish to your diet. Read below to learn answers to some of the most common questions I hear as a dietitian.

1. **Will a pescatarian diet help me lose weight?**
   While there are many ways a pescatarian diet can help you improve health, it is not a weight-loss diet. Weight is not a controllable behavior. We can, however, support good health by eating balanced, nourishing meals. Adopting a pescatarian diet as part of your lifestyle may lead to improvements in health, including some potential weight loss, but weight loss is not guaranteed or our main goal.

2. **Can I substitute other proteins instead of seafood?**
   Although a true pescatarian diet doesn't include beef, poultry, pork, or other meats, many families enjoy these foods regardless. This book was written to help you adopt the diet, but if you want to swap out seafood for other animal proteins every once in a while, that is okay. In fact, you should not eat seafood every day (see the next question).

3. **Should I eat seafood every day?**
   No. The current recommendation for adults is two to three servings per week (totaling eight to 12 ounces). A pescatarian diet does not require you to include seafood at every meal; in fact, the majority of your meals could be plant based.

4. **Is a pescatarian diet safe?**
   A pescatarian diet is safe for most people, so long as you're aware of which fish contain high levels of mercury. Generally, the higher the fish appears on the food chain, the higher the mercury content. Some of the highest-mercury fish include swordfish, shark, king mackerel, and tilefish. Additionally,

pregnant women should avoid more than six ounces of albacore (white) tuna at a time. Pregnant women should also avoid raw fish to reduce risk of food-borne illness.

5. **Do I have to include eggs or dairy?**
Many people who identify as pescatarians include eggs and dairy, but it is a personal choice. There are limitations for someone with lactose intolerance or an allergy to eggs or dairy. In those cases, there are many alternative products that can be used in recipes as a replacement, such as nut or coconut milks.

6. **Can I get enough protein on a pescatarian diet?**
Yes. Most adults in the United States are easily able to meet the recommended amounts of protein each day. Because a pescatarian diet includes protein from fish and seafood, plant-based protein from various sources, and the option to include eggs and dairy products, there are few concerns about protein intake for those following the diet.

7. **Will I be able to afford the ingredients needed to make these recipes or follow the meal plan?**
These recipes include affordable options that are easy to find in most grocery stores. Some types of seafood can be quite expensive, but these recipes are built around fresh or frozen fillets of commonly available fish or canned options for tuna and salmon. There are also tips included for ingredient substitutions if you are unable to find or purchase ingredients called for in a recipe. And because a pescatarian diet doesn't require seafood in every meal, you can stretch your grocery budget further by relying on plant-based meals when you choose to skip seafood.

8. **How much time will I have to spend cooking?**
Many of the recipes can be made in 30 minutes or less and are labeled as such. If you have even less time, look for the Quick Prep label for meals that require little or no active cooking and take 10 minutes or less to prepare. Some meals, such as slow cooker meals and recipes that need time to chill or freeze, may take longer overall, but the active preparation time will not be long.

9. **How can I make a pescatarian diet more family friendly?**
Introducing any new foods to family meals can be challenging. However, these recipes feature familiar flavors and can be easily modified to fit your family's tastes. Seafood is safe to introduce to infants 6 to 12 months of age, but if you have concerns about food allergies or your child is prone to them, please consult with your pediatrician and dietitian first. As for serving

family-friendly pescatarian meals, you can plate ingredients separately, use spices and seasonings more sparingly, or offer dipping sauces or other condiments to appeal to the tastes of younger children. For more information on family meals, I recommend resources by Ellyn Satter, including her Division of Responsibilities model of family feeding.

10. **Will a pescatarian diet harm the environment?**
    If you are conscious about selecting a variety of sustainably caught or farmed seafood, the inclusion of seafood to your diet should not negatively impact the environment. See the section on Ecofriendly Fish (page 20) for more information to guide your decisions.

PORTIONS

A balanced pescatarian plate is very similar to the recommendations from MyPlate (the USDA visual food guide that replaces the food pyramid), which consists of half fruits and vegetables, a quarter protein, and a quarter grain or starch. Please refer to the chart below. I recommend building your plate according to your hunger, meaning that portion sizes will vary. As a starting point, you may want to consider four to five ounces of seafood (in alignment with the recommendation for eight or more ounces per week) or other protein, several servings of fresh or cooked vegetables (½ cup per serving), and one cup of your chosen grain or starch.

THE PROPERLY PORTIONED PESCATARIAN PLATE

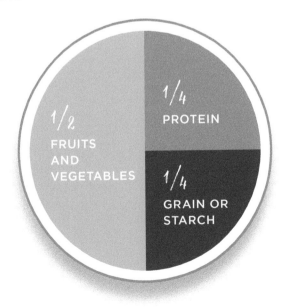

GOOD HEALTH COMES FROM THE SEA

Pescatarians often have the reputation of being very health conscious. In fact, an interest in health and wellness is what first introduces many people to this style of eating. A diet rich in seafood has been part of cultures throughout the world for thousands of years. We now have evidence from a growing body of nutrition science that including seafood in our diets can lead to better health and an improved quality of life as we age.

There is growing concern over health issues like insulin resistance and inflammation, which are at the root of chronic conditions such as type 2 diabetes, cardiovascular disease, certain cancers, and cognitive decline. We know diet plays an important role in overall well-being. A pescatarian diet can provide the nutrients necessary to manage or prevent some of the most serious and costly health conditions that are common in the United States today. Following are a few ways that a pescatarian diet may improve your health.

10 REASONS WHY A PESCATARIAN DIET IS HEALTHY

I think of a healthy diet as something that provides not only essential nutrition, but also satisfaction and great taste. Here are some of the benefits I see in a pescatarian lifestyle.

1. **Brain Health:** Fish is a rich source of EPA and DHA, the fatty acids that can be protective for brain health in adults and support healthy brain development in infants and children.

2. **Blood Pressure:** Consuming fish and seafood on a regular basis has been associated with lower blood pressure in adults, which reduces the risk of heart disease.

3. **Triglycerides:** Research also supports fish in a heart-healthy diet because pescatarian diets have been shown to decrease triglyceride levels.

4. **Saturated Fat:** When compared with the typical American diet, a pescatarian diet is usually lower in saturated fat. Although total fat intake remains similar, a higher percentage comes from mono- and polyunsaturated fatty acids, which are less inflammatory than omega-6 fatty acids from other food sources.

5. **Vitamin D:** Adding two or three servings of fish per week can increase intake of vitamin D. Salmon is one of the few foods that naturally contain vitamin D, an important vitamin for good health.

6. **Iodine:** More people turn to sea salt for cooking and flavoring meals, but this isn't necessarily a healthier choice. Sodium content remains the same, and they miss out on iodine because sea salt is not iodized as most table salts are. Seafood is considered a great source of iodine.

7. **Fiber:** With so many fruits, vegetables, whole grains, and legumes, a pescatarian diet is usually higher in fiber than a typical American diet. This can support good gut health, which often helps with improved regularity or a decrease in uncomfortable GI-related symptoms.

8. **Satiety and Satisfaction:** The combination of protein, fat, and fiber helps you feel full after eating, which may help alleviate hunger between meals and reduce fluctuations in energy levels. When following a pescatarian diet, these nutrients are present in most meals in balanced ratios, helping you walk away from meals feeling truly satisfied.

9. **Sustainability and Practicality:** A pescatarian diet is very flexible and can be easily adapted based on your tastes and preferences. Evidence shows that restrictive diets are not sustainable long term, so having more choices means you might be more successful at creating a realistic lifestyle you can maintain without feeling deprived.

10. **High-Quality, Complete Nutrition:** Vegan and vegetarian diets that eliminate all or most animal products can create nutrition gaps, leading to potential health concerns. A pescatarian diet that includes fish and seafood, as well as the option for eggs and dairy, is a more flexible approach that offers good or excellent sources of essential nutrients.

LOSING WEIGHT

Although many people initially become interested in a pescatarian diet for weight-loss benefits, it is not the main goal. Weight is not a behavior, so there is no guarantee that you will lose weight if you choose to adopt a pescatarian diet. A "diet" is simply the kinds of food a person habitually eats. The evidence shows that regardless of how it's accomplished, any diet pattern that results in a calorie deficit can lead to weight loss. However, that's often at the sacrifice of essential nutrients, and as a dietitian, I do not recommend restrictive diets of any type. Health and well-being is always a higher priority. Both can be improved with a balanced, sustainable diet pattern, and I believe that the pescatarian diet does just that. Here are some additional tips to remember if you wish to improve your health through a pescatarian diet.

1. **Don't think of it as a diet.** Reject the idea that you're on a diet. Diets are temporary and can be harmful to your relationship with food and your body. Our goal in this book is to supply the important nutrition you need for good health and happiness. It's flexible and adaptable so no matter where you are, in any situation, you can select foods that align with your lifestyle.

2. **Variety is key.** Including a wide variety of foods in your diet ensures you not only get the nutrition your body needs but that you don't get bored of the same routine day after day. Variety can come in the form of different ingredients, but you might also enjoy preparing familiar ingredients in new or creative ways. This makes for a richer eating experience that allows you to practice mindfulness, something that is helpful for those wishing to make lasting lifestyle changes that align with their values.

3. **Focus on foods you truly enjoy.** You must be satisfied to be truly satiated! It's about more than physical fullness; by choosing foods you genuinely

enjoy and want to eat, you can discover satisfaction that lets you reduce intense cravings or a desire to eat out of boredom.

4. **Tune into your hunger and fullness.** Many of us go through years of dieting, and over time, we become disconnected from the signals our body is sending about whether we feel hungry or full. Rather than ignoring or numbing your hunger, try to think of it as the way your body is communicating with you. Honoring your hunger and respecting your fullness are two key principles of intuitive eating. Doing so allows you to adjust your meals or eating schedule to avoid feeling hungry between meals and snacks.

5. **Make your meals mindful.** Practicing mindful eating habits and slowing down during mealtimes gives you an opportunity to connect with the experience of eating. It can help you cultivate awareness of your food likes and dislikes, so instead of mindlessly finishing a meal you don't enjoy, you can determine whether you like something enough to finish the serving. You may also notice when you feel full before you hit the point of being uncomfortably stuffed. Over time, you will learn to respect your fullness and trust that your body has been adequately nourished.

THE SCIENCE

Although few studies isolate a pescatarian diet to examine health benefits, many studies on individual nutrients found within a pescatarian diet are available. Omega-3 fatty acids are among the most highly studied nutrients of all, so we have a good understanding of the role they play in human health. There is also substantial research investigating the benefits of vegetarian or semi-vegetarian diets that provides more information on the impacts of adding fish and seafood to an otherwise plant-based diet. A pescatarian diet is generally viewed as nutritionally complete and deemed to be a healthy style of eating when compared with other dietary patterns. Here's how some of the science breaks down when it comes to these topics:

Omega-3s: Omega-3 fatty acids are a type of unsaturated fat. Although also found in plants, including nuts and seeds, the form found in animals and particularly seafood is preferred for human consumption. It boasts higher bioavailability, or the degree to which the body can efficiently use it for important bodily functions. The research shows it to be particularly beneficial for having a protective effect against heart disease and cognitive decline. Omega-3s from low-mercury seafood can also support a healthy pregnancy and brain and neurodevelopment in infants and children.

Mercury: Mercury is found in low or trace amounts in most fish. It is ingested as part of their natural diets and accumulates in the flesh. When ingested in high amounts, it can also accumulate in humans and lead to neurotoxic effects. However, the guidelines to consume eight to 12 ounces of fish per week are established as safe levels of intake. Advisories are also issued through state and local health departments and the EPA (U.S. Environmental Protection Agency). Consult these sources to see if there is concern for high mercury levels in local or domestic fish.

Dairy: The inclusion of dairy in a pescatarian or plant-based diet is optional. For those with lactose intolerance or dairy allergies, it is best to eliminate dairy or find low-lactose or dairy-free alternatives to replace traditional dairy products. Dairy can play a positive role in human health, providing essential nutrients such as calcium, potassium, phosphorus, vitamins A, D, and B12, riboflavin, and niacin. Research shows that including low-fat dairy in your diet may prevent osteoporosis and fractures, reduce risk of type 2 diabetes, and potentially lower risk of cardiometabolic disease.

Celiac disease and gluten intolerance: Celiac disease is an autoimmune condition in which the body creates an inflammatory response when gluten from wheat or wheat products is present in the diet. Gluten intolerances may fall under a broader category of food intolerances, referred to as FODMAPs (Fermentable Oligo-, Di-, Mono-saccharides And Polyols). This can cause similar gastrointestinal symptoms, poor digestion and absorption of nutrients, and other symptoms. Celiac disease occurs in about 1 percent of adults. While it is rare, it does require a lifelong avoidance of gluten to manage symptoms. Fortunately, many ingredients and foods in a pescatarian diet are naturally gluten-free. Items such as traditional breads, wheat tortillas and wraps, crackers, or pastas and wheat-based grains are not allowed, but many alternatives exist.

While the potential health benefits of a pescatarian diet are evident, I urge you to keep in mind that a healthy, sustainable diet is one that you enjoy and that is supported by your lifestyle and goals. I don't think of a pescatarian diet as a diet at all, but rather an overall way of eating that includes nourishing foods, mindfulness, pleasure, and creativity in the kitchen. Now that you understand the basics of a pescatarian diet, in the next chapter we will explore the culinary practices that can help you create delicious seafood recipes at home.

— 2 —

THE FOOD-LOVER'S PESCATARIAN KITCHEN

ESSENTIAL PESCATARIAN INGREDIENTS

It is wonderful to have a variety of food options, but I know it can feel overwhelming to have too wide of a selection. In an effort to help, I narrowed it down to the most reliable ingredients that appear on many of my grocery lists. These are kitchen staples you can find year-round, with a few exceptions, that are easily found at most major retailers throughout the United States. When you keep these items on hand in your kitchen, you will always be able to throw together a nourishing meal in a pinch. Let's discuss these essential ingredients and where you should store them.

REFRIGERATOR

The most highly perishable ingredients should be stored in the refrigerator to prevent spoiling. I keep my refrigerator organized so I know what I have on hand at all times with a simple glance. This allows me to use ingredients before they hit their expiration date. Items you should store in the refrigerator include:

* Perishable produce such as leafy greens, fresh fruit, and pre-chopped or prepared vegetables
* Dairy products such as milk, butter, cheese, yogurt, cottage cheese, and kefir, or dairy-free alternatives
* Fresh herbs
* Fresh fish and seafood or thawed frozen fish and seafood
* Condiments and cooking ingredients such as lemon juice, lime juice, soy sauce, and mayonnaise

PANTRY

Your pantry should be stocked with items purchased in bulk and other less perishable items. I also like to keep some convenient options on hand for when I need to whip up a meal in a short amount of time. Items you should store in the pantry include:

* Canned fish and seafood such as tuna, salmon, smoked oysters, and anchovies
* Shelf-stable produce such as potatoes (sweet and white), avocados, and onions
* Canned tomato paste (no salt added) or low-sodium pasta sauce
* Canned beans and lentils
* Nuts and seeds
* Rice, quinoa, couscous, dry pasta, and oats
* Bread, tortillas, wraps, and crackers
* Ancient grains like freekeh, sorghum, and bulgur
* Dried herbs and spices
* Cooking oils

FREEZER

If you have the space, freezers are a wonderful resource for storing bulk purchases. You can thaw ingredients as needed or safely store leftovers from batch cooking until needed. I will also store nuts in the freezer if I don't use them quickly to avoid letting them become rancid. Other freezer items include:

* Frozen vegetables
* Frozen fruit
* Frozen fish fillets
* Frozen shrimp, cooked or uncooked
* Batch-cooked meals or leftovers

NOTE: There are many opportunities to incorporate seasonal ingredients like fruit, vegetables, herbs, and seafood. These items are often less expensive when in season, with improved quality and taste. Look for these when available if you wish to, but remember that you can still rely on trusted kitchen staples to make these recipes.

FLAVORFUL FISH

I often hear people comment on the lack of flavor in fish or the overly "fishy" taste. Neither bodes well for convincing them to include seafood more often. Thankfully, there are many methods for creating a dish that appeals to any palate, whether you prefer something mild and balanced or bold and well seasoned. Here are my top tips for flavoring fish:

PICK A PERFECT PAIR

1. **Know your ingredients.** Understand the difference between fish, mollusks, and crustaceans to choose ingredients or cooking methods that will yield the best results. Think of your seafood selections in terms of texture (delicate, medium, or firm) and flavor (mild, moderate, or full), especially when looking for recipe substitutions.

2. **Incorporate acids and seasonings.** Acidic components (citrus, vinegar, wine, or pickled ingredients) and seasonings (herbs and spices) liven up your cooking. The more savory a dish, the more it needs something to perk it up. Acid is one of the basic tastes, so it takes priority for me, but adding seasonings takes a dish from good to great.

3. **Choose sides that complement but don't compete.** Finally, keep your entrée as the star of the show by choosing side dishes that play a supporting role. A pescatarian menu should feature many vegetables, greens, and grains, but too much variety can be overwhelming. Keep it simple: Focus on quality over quantity.

CREATE FULL-ON FLAVOR

1. **Fat carries flavor.** Fatty fish are like the dark meat of the seafood world. Compared with whitefish, they contain more flavor and omega-3 fatty acids. But they also need a different seasoning strategy since fat can dull our perception of other flavors. Try experimenting with more acid or serve with a hearty starch.

2. **Don't fear the saltshaker.** Highly processed foods and restaurant recipes have left us wary of sodium. But most ingredients for home cooking are naturally low in sodium. Salt enhances other ingredients in your finished dishes.

3. **Try different cooking methods.** Smoking, grilling, and baking fish yield very different flavors. Experiment with how you prepare your favorite fish to refresh your routine.

4. **Crank the heat.** No, not the spice level! Simply try to serve your hot entrées hot. As food cools, it's less likely to carry aromas into your mouth and nasal cavity. By serving your meal immediately, you enhance your awareness of flavor without adding a single ingredient.

5. **Season early.** Flavor blooms in a dish when elements cook together. You can create more balance between salt, fat, acidity, and sweetness when you introduce seasonings earlier in the cooking process versus adding just before serving.

6. **Keep an open mind.** You may see ingredients in these recipes that make you question whether they belong. But heat, acid, and time change how flavors interact, so don't be afraid to experiment. Trust your taste buds to let you know whether it's worth repeating.

7. **Savor the moment.** Mindfulness is often the final ingredient needed to create harmony in a meal. Regardless of how a dish is prepared or seasoned, tuning in to your enjoyment of the eating experience leaves a lasting impression.

ESSENTIAL PESCATARIAN EQUIPMENT

A common myth is that you need a fully stocked, appliance-filled kitchen to cook great meals at home. That couldn't be further from the truth. These essential pieces of kitchen equipment allow you to prepare balanced, nourishing meals without needing to invest in expensive equipment or cluttering up your kitchen. There are pieces in the "nice-to-have" category, such as slow cookers, food processors, blenders, and other pieces that make cooking more convenient or fun, but I've narrowed it down to the "need-to-have" pieces that will help you successfully prepare pescatarian meals. A few recipes in the book will use those nice-to-haves, but you can make most pescatarian meals without them. Specifically, if you have a large baking dish, a 9-inch-square baking pan, a food processor, a blender, and a hand mixer or stand mixer, and a kitchen thermometer in addition to the items below, you should easily be able to make every single recipe in the book.

1. **Sharp Knife and Cutting Boards:** I consider these at the top of the list because you need them for every meal you prepare. I can't overstate how important it is to have a knife you know and trust. Take time to explore options and find one that feels comfortable for you to use. Then make sure you maintain it well by keeping it sharpened. A dull knife is more dangerous because it's more likely to slip and slide as you're using it, increasing the risk of cutting yourself. I also recommend having at least two good knives and cutting boards so you can prepare ingredients on separate cutting boards, as that will minimize the risk of cross-contamination and foodborne illnesses.

2. **Rimmed Baking Sheets:** My baking sheet is the ultimate workhorse in my kitchen because of its versatility. It can be used for the obvious baking needs, but also for baking fish for sheet pan meals, roasting vegetables, toasting nuts, and much more. The rimmed versions help contain messes and can usually be found for an affordable price. Be sure to look for a durable option that resists warping, like a thick, heavy-gauge aluminum, or you may find your recipes cook unevenly in the oven.

3. **Large and Small Nonstick Pan or Cast Iron Skillet and Small Saucepan:** These pieces are key to creating one-pan meals where all ingredients can be cooked simultaneously, which can save you a lot of time. I love my cast iron skillet because it's well seasoned and heats very evenly, but it is heavy to move around. If you prefer a lower-maintenance option, nonstick skillets are my preference over stainless steel. They're easier to clean and require less oil for cooking. A small saucepan is great for preparing sauces and soups and for cooking in smaller portions.

4. **Mixing Bowl Set:** I consider these essential based on how often I use them. They serve me well for mixing, stirring, whipping, dredging, thawing, and, in a pinch, serving. Having a set with multiple sizes gives you options when cooking for a crowd versus serving up a smaller meal.

5. **Versatile Utensils:** It's up to you how much you want to include in this category. I make sure I have a full set of measuring cups and measuring spoons. I also include pieces like a spatula, slotted spoon, and sauce spoon, plus a pair of tongs for mixing salads and grilling or roasting and a peeler for potatoes and carrots. Many of these serve multiple purposes so you can get by with only a few, so long as you're okay with doing the dishes more often.

ECOFRIENDLY FISH

Seafood can be an ethical and sustainable choice, but that does require some knowledge about the industry. There are stark differences between the quality of practices among both wild fisheries and fish farming. It's worth noting that some fishing methods, such as hook-and-line fishing (or trolling) and farmed shellfish, are very sustainable and ecofriendly. Other methods, particularly long-line fishing and dredging or bottom trawling, create a significant amount of bycatch: when sea life other than the targeted species is accidentally caught by long lines or captured in fishing nets. Look for commercial fisheries that are taking responsible steps to limit bycatch and use fishing methods that minimize disruption to the ecosystem.

In addition to the environmental impact, seafood fraud is also a growing concern. Wild-caught fish often changes hands many times along the supply chain, and mislabeling and fraud are becoming more common. I mention these concerns not to deter your from enjoying a pescatarian diet, but simply to inform you of some considerations to keep in mind. Here are five things you can do to be a smart shopper when it comes to selecting seafood:

1. **Do your homework.** As you plan recipes or make a shopping list, take time to learn about the seafood available in your area. I recommend checking out the Resources section (page 155) to find information to guide your purchases. You can learn which species are at risk of overfishing (or are currently overfished) and choose accordingly from the recommended species whose populations are at safe levels.

2. **Shop locally when you can.** "Local" for many Americans means buying domestically caught or farmed seafood. This lessens the environmental impact by reducing how far seafood is shipped to

reach your market and can support companies who practice sustainable fishing or farming methods in U.S. fisheries.

3. **Ask questions.** Don't be shy about asking the fishmonger or market manager questions when buying fresh fish. They are the most knowledgeable about their selection. Many people don't realize seafood is seasonal like many other ingredients, so be conscious of what is available when you're shopping. The fishmonger should also know which fishing methods were used and can make a recommendation for a more environmentally friendly catch. They can also guide you toward a sustainable choice, such as smaller or less popular fish that can still work well for your chosen recipe.

4. **Portions (and size) matter.** Although we are accustomed to large serving sizes, especially for protein, we can enjoy the recommended amount of fish and seafood without resorting to large portions. A pescatarian diet provides many options to fill your plate with vegetables, grains, or other side dishes so you feel full and satisfied.

5. **Work to minimize food waste.** Use the Prep and Storage tips (page 25) I share to properly store your seafood once you get it home. Many of us waste food unintentionally, and being more conscious of how we shop can reduce the amount of food that ends up in the trash.

Grilled Swordfish with Chimichurri & Roasted Vegetables, page 98

THE PESCATARIAN'S GUIDE TO SEAFOOD

When you're new to cooking with seafood, it can be a little uncomfortable. That's alright! I always encourage the families I work with to keep cooking creative and carefree if they can—even if mistakes happen, you can usually salvage the meal or learn from them. To reduce the risk of that happening, I'm sharing some of my top tips to get you started on the right foot as you begin cooking with fish and seafood.

PICKING SEAFOOD

1. **Assess your kitchen and take inventory.** Before purchasing a single ingredient, I like to scan my fridge, pantry, and freezer to account for what I already have. Better yet, take a picture with your phone to reference when you are food shopping. This way you can avoid purchasing too much, and you'll make sure you have room to store everything once you get it back home.

2. **Plan your schedule.** If you know you'll be cooking your fish or seafood in the next day or so, purchasing fresh is a great option. However, if you need to wait longer, it might be preferable to purchase frozen seafood so you can thaw it when you're ready to cook.

3. **Do a little homework.** Refer to the Resources (page 155) in the back of this book for up-to-date information on fish and seafood. Learn which species or brands to avoid purchasing and which types of seafood are currently in season or available in your region.

4. **Trust your nose.** Fresh fish should smell like it just came from the sea: mild, without a strong aroma. If you notice a fishy smell or sour, ammonia-like smell, assume the fish is past its prime.

5. **For fresh fillets or steaks:** Ask to touch the fish before purchasing or have the fishmonger do this for you. There should be some spring in the flesh, and it should appear moist and clean and show no discoloration or drying around the edges. If purchasing packaged fresh fish, examine the packaging to look for time and temperature indicators. This lets you know the fish was handled properly and stored at the correct temperature.

6. **For shellfish:** Sacks or containers of fresh shellfish should have a tag with a label. This will tell you how the shellfish was harvested and from where, and you can locate the processor's certification number to verify the safety and quality of the shellfish if needed. Avoid or discard any oysters, clams, or mussels with cracked or broken shells.

7. **When purchasing frozen:** Frozen fish is often viewed as lower quality than fresh, but in regions far from the coast, the quality may actually be comparable to or better than fresh fish. Use the same general rules for judging frozen fish based on appearance. Reach for packages that are toward the bottom or back of a freezer case because they are less likely to have experienced thawing and refreezing. Ice crystals inside the package aren't a good sign.

8. **When purchasing canned, pouched, or preserved fish in tins:** Read labels for information on how the seafood is packed (in water versus in oil) and the sustainability standards used for fishing. As with other food labels, it can be hard to distinguish the validity of labels that use vague terms like "wild-caught" or "sustainably caught." You're better off verifying the species and fishing methods to determine whether it is an ethical and environmentally friendly choice.

9. **If all else fails, substitute:** Finally, don't be afraid to break free from a recipe and make ingredient substitutions. When a recipe calls for an oily fish, like salmon, you can generally find another oily fish that is comparable. The same goes for whitefish. In fact, some recipes may not even specify which variety of fish should be used. You'll grow more confident in altering recipes the more you cook, so the first step is to simply get started!

PREP AND STORAGE

1. Whether storing fresh fish or thawing from frozen, refrigerate on the bottom shelf below other ingredients. You don't want your other food exposed to water or drippings from raw seafood, so always cover the container and make sure it is sealed to prevent leaks.

2. Store your fresh fish in the same package and wrapping your fishmonger uses if you plan to cook it within one or two days. I recommend using it within that time for optimal freshness, but if you need to store it longer than that, place it in a zip-top bag, press to remove the air, and place the sealed bag surrounded by ice in a colander. Set the colander in a large mixing bowl, and store in the refrigerator until ready to cook.

3. Be mindful of changes in temperature. Keep fresh fish chilled at a constant temperature (below 40°F), and avoid letting frozen fish thaw and refreeze. Be on the lookout for freezer burn on frozen fish, as well; it will look like a light or discolored area and appear very dry or with ice crystals present.

4. Thawing frozen seafood is best done gradually by transferring it to the refrigerator and allowing it to thaw overnight. If you need to thaw more quickly, a best practice is to seal it in a plastic bag (if not already inside sealed plastic) and set in cold water. As a last resort, frozen fish can be defrosted in the microwave. Set the microwave to the defrost setting, and check every 90 seconds. Remove when the fish is still icy but beginning to soften.

5. Cook thawed fish as soon as possible after thawing to preserve the quality of the fish and maintain good food safety practices. Remember that freezing does not kill all parasites and pathogens, so cooking fish is still recommended as the safest way to enjoy fish at home.

6. Always practice good hand hygiene and food safety when handling raw or frozen seafood. Wash hands often, and keep cutting boards and utensils used to prepare raw seafood separate from other ingredients.

7. Whitefish like tilapia, cod, or halibut can be cooked from frozen when needed. If you have an evening where you just don't have the time to do a lot of prep work, frozen fillets can be pulled straight from the freezer and placed on a sheet pan to bake.

8. Fillets may still contain pinbones if the fishmonger hasn't already removed them. Take a pair of needle-nose pliers and lay the fillet skin-side down. Locate the pinbones just under the surface, and gently press down around them until you can grab them with the pliers. Give the pinbone a tug to remove it, then repeat until all bones are removed. One trick to speed up this process is to turn a small mixing bowl upside down and drape the fillet over the bowl. This exposes the pinbones and makes them easier to find.

9. Before cooking, gently rinse fish under cold running water. Pat dry before placing in a pan or on a grill top or sheet pan to cook.

10. If using a marinade to season seafood, discard any leftovers. Any ingredients or utensils that come in contact with raw seafood should not be used with cooked seafood or other ready-to-eat ingredients. If you need some of the marinade to baste your recipe or make a sauce, be sure to reserve enough before adding your raw seafood. Marinating should always take place in the refrigerator, never on the countertop or at room temperature.

COOKING METHODS AND BEST PRACTICES

When someone mentions they don't eat seafood often, I usually ask, "Why not?" Food preferences aside, the most common answer is that they're not sure how to cook it. Despite their reputation for being difficult to cook, I find fish and seafood are among the simplest and fastest proteins to prepare. Here are a few of the most common cooking methods that can get you great results with home cooking:

Pan Roasting: Pan roasting is similar to panfrying in that a shallow pan coated with oil serves as the cooking surface. It's considered a dry-heat method and can be a good option for fish or seafood, especially if preparing one-skillet meals or pan roasting other ingredients. Start with medium heat for evenly cooked fish that doesn't become too dry or flaky.

Oven Roasting: Roasting in the oven occurs at temperatures above 150°F. It is also a dry-heat cooking method, meaning the flavor of the fish or seafood is enhanced while cooking without relying on a sauce, stew, or gravy. Start with oven temperatures around 350°F, and make adjustments to time and temperature based on your recipe and the size of the fish you're preparing.

Poaching: Poaching uses a liquid to simmer the fish in a shallow pan. It can be a very quick cooking process, sometimes taking no more than 10 minutes. Poaching adds flavor without adding extra fat. It's a good fit for less oily whitefish, such as tilapia, cod, halibut, or snapper, but it could also work for salmon and trout. Use a slotted spatula or fish turner, as the cooked fish may easily flake apart in the poaching liquid.

Searing: Searing occurs over high heat on a flat surface. It creates a caramelized crust and, when done properly, should not cause sticking or burning to the pan. Salmon, shrimp, tuna, and swordfish steaks are commonly prepared using this dry-heat cooking method.

Steaming: Steaming helps preserve the natural moisture in seafood and is a good fit for delicate seafood that may not stand up to more aggressive cooking techniques. This moist-heat cooking method is often used for shellfish, like clams and mussels, or crustaceans.

Grilling: Grilling is another dry-heat cooking method, and one that often leads to sticking. Coating your grill grates with a high–smoke point oil can help prevent this. Most fish can cook directly over the grates on a grill but can easily fall apart, so use care when flipping or turning.

Meat Thermometer: A meat thermometer is the most accurate way to tell when fish is finished cooking. For most fish, cooking to 140 to 145°F is a safe level that doesn't sacrifice the texture or flavor of the cooked dish. If you don't have a meat thermometer, look for an opaque color and firm, flaky texture to determine when your fish is finished cooking.

I hope this chapter has armed you with the vital information you need to be a conscientious fish consumer and buyer. Although there is a lot of information here, you now know how to create delicious pescatarian recipes at home. To make it even easier, we are now going to go over a three-week pescatarian meal plan that you can use at home. I'm so excited to show you, so let's get started!

BOWL BUILDER

One of my favorite food quotes by the late Anthony Bourdain says, "Good food is very often, even most often, simple food." And I'm all about simple when it comes to cooking. I'll confess I eat most of my meals out of bowls for that very reason. There's something comforting (and convenient) about enjoying a satisfying meal out of a single dish.

Popular bowl-style meals like Buddha Bowls and Nourish Bowls are prime examples of how assembling ingredients into a bowl provides a balanced meal. In our case, bowl-style meals can catch any leftover ingredients to create quick-and-easy meals and reduce food waste, no recipe required!

START WITH THIS SIMPLE SERVING SIZE GUIDE:

- Protein: four to five ounces of fish or seafood

- Vegetables: Remember ½ cup equals one serving, so select a variety of vegetables or use multiple servings of the same vegetable to add two to three servings (1 to 1½ cups total)

- Leafy greens: Start with 1 to 2 loosely packed cups per bowl. You can always add more.

- Beans or lentils: ½ cup

- Cheese, yogurt, or sauce: up to ¼ cup

You're now ready to use this template to quickly build your bowl with the staple ingredients you already have. See some of my favorite combinations here:

Taco Bowl: Start with a base of chopped romaine lettuce. Use leftover grilled or blackened fish as your protein, or to avoid cooking, open a can of salmon or tuna or thaw precooked shrimp. Then add black beans, salsa, or diced tomatoes, avocado or a scoop of sour cream, and garnish with chili powder, cilantro, or a chili-lime spice blend.

Hearty Grain Bowl: Start by reheating a cooked grain, such as rice, quinoa, couscous, or your favorite ancient grain. Layer a serving of fresh spinach on top to wilt. Add roasted or raw veggies, such as broccoli, onions, carrots, or zucchini. Top with a serving of fish or seafood (canned or cooked), and drizzle with olive oil or an oil-based sauce, such as leftover pesto sauce or chimichurri.

Kitchen-Sink Veggie Bowl: Just like it sounds, this hash-style bowl can use up any spare ingredients you may have. Chop any raw veggies into small cubes and quickly pan roast with your favorite cooking oil. Season with a spice blend, such as Italian herbs, curry powder, or Mexican spices. Add a can of black beans, chickpeas, or canned lentils (drained and rinsed) and heat through. Place in a bowl, then top with a fried or over-easy egg and a drizzle of hot sauce, soy sauce, or other seasoning.

Satisfying Salad Bowl: Sometimes salads get a bad reputation for not being hearty or filling enough for a meal. Start with your favorite mixed greens, arugula, or massaged kale. Then add other ingredients, making sure to include a protein source and something chewy, crunchy, savory, and sweet, such as dried fruit. Top with oil and vinegar for a simple dressing or use leftover sauces from other recipes.

Spring Greens Panzanella Salad with Shrimp, page 64

PESCATARIAN MEAL PLANNING

THE JOYS OF MEAL PLANNING

I approach meal planning as an act of self-care. When I have a plan, I waste less food, spend less time in the kitchen, and create a less stressful life. These meal plans are meant to be a flexible guide to show you how to mix and match these recipes to fit your lifestyle. Most of the effort is done for you, so scan through the shopping lists, make adjustments to the recipes, and enjoy the process!

LEFTOVERS

1. **Declutter Your Kitchen.** Storing and accessing leftover meals is made more challenging when your space is cluttered. Take a few minutes to organize your shelves or drawers in the fridge so you can easily see what you have.

2. **Get the Right Tools.** Invest in a set of quality food storage containers with matching lids. I recommend having multiple sizes so you have options no matter how much or how little is left. Keep food storage bags and aluminum foil or plastic wrap handy as well.

3. **Cool It Down.** Heat from cooking will create condensation inside a sealed container, which may leave your leftovers soggy and unappetizing. Let your recipe cool down before covering and placing in the refrigerator. Be sure not to leave food out more than two hours, though.

4. **Label Your Freezer Meals.** Forgotten food is wasted food, so keep tabs on what needs to be used sooner (rather than later) with labels. Mark the date the food was prepared or a "use by" date three to six months in the future. There's no perfect system, so find what helps you remember to use what you've already worked to prepare.

5. **Let It Go.** As disappointing as it is to throw away uneaten food, eating food past its prime is not worth it. If you feel like leftovers are questionable, check for off-putting odors or a slimy, watery texture that indicates spoilage.

AFTER THE THREE WEEKS

Once you make it through these suggested meal plans, you're well on your way to adopting a pescatarian lifestyle. It's one that can support good health, fit into your busy routine, and perhaps most importantly, help you discover how foods make you feel. I'll leave you with these additional reminders.

Embrace a lifestyle, not a diet. A classic hallmark of a "diet" is a start point and end point. But a true lifestyle can grow and adapt with you through any season of life. Focus on making sustainable changes that support your goals and priorities.

Make it your own. Keep in mind that everyone's needs and preferences differ. Although most recipes are written to serve four to six, use these first few weeks to assess how filling and satisfying they are for you. In the future, you may need to increase or decrease the portions to better fit your appetite.

Keep an open mind. It's normal to try a recipe or ingredient for the first time and not love it. It may take multiple attempts and adjustments to land on something you enjoy. Don't be shy about altering these meals plans to reflect your preferences.

Be kind to yourself. It's easy to feel like you've failed on a diet. Since a pescatarian lifestyle isn't a diet, you don't have to limit yourself to black-and-white thinking. Use this time to practice mindful eating, reconnect to your hunger and fullness, and discover the many ways food can nourish your body to help you feel your best.

Stay curious. If you want to learn more about the benefits of a pescatarian diet, consider working with a registered dietitian who can support you in aligning this lifestyle with your personal health needs. You can also continue learning more about sustainability and sourcing of seafood to choose ingredients and brands you feel good about supporting.

PANTRY AND FRIDGE STAPLES

Consider these ingredients staples that you routinely keep on hand. They serve as your trusted options for cooking oils, condiments, seasonings, and spices. Replace items as needed.

* Allspice, ground
* Baking powder
* Baking soda
* Balsamic glaze
* Basil, dried
* Black pepper
* Bread crumbs, whole-wheat
* Brown rice syrup (or maple syrup)
* Butter
* Capers
* Cardamom, ground
* Cayenne pepper, ground
* Chili powder
* Chinese five-spice powder
* Chocolate chips, mini
* Cinnamon, ground
* Cornstarch
* Cranberries, dried
* Creamy peanut butter
* Cumin, ground
* Curry powder
* Dijon mustard
* Dill, dried
* Flour, all-purpose
* Garlic powder
* Ginger, ground
* Half-and-half
* Heavy (whipping) cream
* Honey

* Jamaican jerk seasoning
* Mayonnaise
* Milk, 2%
* Mustard powder
* Oil, canola
* Oil, extra-virgin olive
* Old Bay seasoning (low-sodium if available)
* Olives, Kalamata
* Onion powder
* Oregano, dried
* Panko bread crumbs
* Paprika
* Red curry paste
* Red pepper flakes
* Sage, dried
* Salt
* Sesame oil
* Smoked paprika
* Soy sauce, low-sodium
* Sriracha or hot sauce
* Sugar, brown
* Sugar, granulated
* Tahini
* Vanilla extract
* Vegetable stock, low-sodium
* Vinegar, apple cider
* Vinegar, balsamic
* Vinegar, red wine

WEEK 1 SUGGESTED MEAL PLAN

	BREAKFAST	LUNCH	DINNER
M	Breakfast Mason Jars (page 53)	Smashed Chickpea Salad Sandwiches (page 85)	Thai Dye Bowls with Freekeh (page 80)
T	Breakfast Mason Jars (page 53) (leftovers)	Smashed Chickpea Salad Sandwiches (page 85) (leftovers)	Spicy Shakshuka Breakfast-for-Dinner Skillet (page 91)
W	Breakfast Mason Jars (page 53) or Spicy Shakshuka Breakfast-for-Dinner Skillet (page 91) (leftovers)	Breakfast Mason Jars (page 53) or Spicy Shakshuka Breakfast-for-Dinner Skillet (page 91) (leftovers)	Thai Dye Bowls with Freekeh (page 80) (leftovers)
T	Breakfast Mason Jars (page 53) or Spicy Shakshuka Breakfast-for-Dinner Skillet (page 91) (leftovers)	Breakfast Mason Jars (page 53) or Spicy Shakshuka Breakfast-for-Dinner Skillet (page 91) (leftovers)	Mediterranean Salmon Wraps (page 97)
F	Breakfast Mason Jars (page 53) (leftovers)	Thai Dye Bowls with Freekeh (page 80) (leftovers)	Green Bean Niçoise Salad with Tuna (page 67)
S	Zucchini Pancakes with Smoked Salmon (page 55) (freeze leftovers)	Mediterranean Salmon Wraps (page 97) (leftovers)	Thai Dye Bowls with Freekeh (page 80) (leftovers)
S	Savory Potato Frittata with Smoked Trout (page 59)	Green Bean Niçoise Salad with Tuna (page 67) (leftovers)	Creamy Cod Piccata with Spaghetti Squash (page 112)

	SNACKS	SIDES
+	No-Bake Fruit & Seed Granola Bars (page 135) and apple slices Curry Tuna Salad Snackers (page 132) (to be eaten throughout the week)	Massaged Kale Salad with Sesame-Lime Dressing (can be made in a larger batch and enjoyed throughout the week) (page 66)

Breakfast Mason Jars (page 53): Make four breakfasts for the week. Store and chill in mason jars or other sealed food storage containers. If needed, keep ingredients separate and layer before or after reheating.

Cook the freekeh in advance: Cook the freekeh for the Thai Dye Bowls with Freekeh (page 80) on Sunday night, then just reheat when ready to combine with other ingredients for your meal. You can also cut or chop any vegetables needed or prepare the sauce in advance.

No-Bake Fruit & Seed Granola Bars (page 135): Store half the bars in the freezer and half in the fridge until needed.

Make the Massaged Kale Salad with Sesame-Lime Dressing (page 66): If desired, prep the kale salad early in the week and continue adding leftover vegetables or other ingredients to the mix as the week goes on to reduce food waste.

SHOPPING LIST

You may have leftovers of some ingredients. Plan to roll them over to the following week or incorporate them into snacks or other recipes to avoid waste. Don't be shy about making substitutions to use what you already have before purchasing something new.

Many items may be purchased in bulk, in small or large quantities, depending on what you plan to use them for. Shopping in the bulk section can be an economical option because there is no need to pay for labeling or packaging. It can also reduce food waste by allowing you to purchase only as much as you need.

Vegetables

Fresh produce can spoil quickly, so try to avoid over-purchasing whenever possible. If needed, fresh herbs can be swapped for the dried version. Plan to use leftover ingredients as an option for snacks throughout the week or to add more veggies to your entrées and side dishes.

- Alfalfa sprouts (1 container)
- Asparagus (1 small bunch)
- Avocados (2)
- Bell peppers, red (4)
- Carrots, shredded (1 bag)
- Cauliflower (1 head)
- Celery (1 bunch)
- Cucumbers (2)

* Dill, fresh (1 bunch)
* Garlic (1 bulb or jar)
* Green beans (1 pound)
* Kale (1 large bunch)
* Lettuce, romaine (1 head)
* Onion, yellow (1)
* Onions, red (2)
* Parsley, fresh (1 bunch)
* Potatoes, new (½ pound)
* Potatoes, yellow (2)
* Radishes (1 small bunch)
* Red cabbage, shredded (1 bag)
* Scallions (1 bunch)
* Spinach (1 large container)
* Tomato, Roma (1)
* Tomatoes, cherry
  (2 cups or 1 container)
* Zucchini (1 large)

Fruit

* Apples (2 or 3)
* Apricots, dried (½ cup)
* Lemons (2 or 3)
* Limes (1 or 2)

Beans & Legumes

* Chickpeas, 1 (14.5-ounce) can
* Edamame, frozen, shelled (1 bag)
* Hummus (1 container)
* Split peas, green, dry (1¼ cups)

Whole Grains

* Bread, whole-wheat (1 loaf) or wraps (1 package)
* Freekeh, uncooked (1 cup)
* Oats, rolled, uncooked (1½ cups)

Seafood

* Cod, fillets, fresh or frozen, 4 (6-ounce) fillets
* Salmon, 2 (6-ounce) cans
* Salmon, smoked (4 ounces)
* Trout, smoked (8 ounces)
* Tuna, packed in water, 3 (5-ounce) cans

Nuts & Seeds

* Almonds, slivered (½ cup)
* Flaxseed, ground (¼ cup)
* Hemp hearts (1 bag)
* Pepitas (¼ cup)
* Pistachios, shelled (¼ cup)

Dairy & Eggs

* Cheese, goat or feta, crumbled (1 package)
* Cheese, pepper Jack, shredded (1 cup)
* Cheese, provolone or Gouda, sliced (1 package)
* Cream cheese, low-fat (1 block)
* Eggs, large (2 dozen)
* Yogurt, Greek, plain, low-fat (1 container)

Other Items

* Cereal, crisped rice (1 box)
* Chipotles in adobo sauce, 1 (7-ounce) can
* Coconut, unsweetened flakes (1 bag)
* Marinara sauce (1 jar)
* Salsa (1 jar)
* Tofu, firm, 1 (14-ounce) package
* Vegetable stock, low-sodium (1 quart)
* Wine, white (1 bottle)

WEEK 2 SUGGESTED MEAL PLAN

	BREAKFAST	LUNCH	DINNER
M	Savory Potato Fritatta with Smoked Trout (page 59) (leftovers from Week 1)	Creamy Cod Piccata with Spaghetti Squash (page 112) (leftovers from Week 1)	Crispy Chickpea–Stuffed Sweet Potatoes (page 81)
T	Raspberry-Lemon Baked Oatmeal Muffins (page 58) (prep Sunday or Monday night)	Creamy Cod Piccata with Spaghetti Squash (page 112) (leftovers from Week 1)	Sofritas Taco Salad Bowls (page 82)
W	Savory Potato Fritatta with Smoked Trout (page 59) (leftovers from Week 1)	Sofritas Taco Salad Bowls (page 82) (leftovers)	Baked Salmon with Greek Veggies & Avocado Tzatziki (page 118)
T	Ginger-Berry Smoothie (page 51)	Creamy Cod Piccata with Spaghetti Squash (page 112) (leftovers from Week 1)	White Bean & Kale Skillet with Quick-Fried Egg (page 89)
F	Raspberry-Lemon Baked Oatmeal Muffins (page 58) (leftovers)	White Bean & Kale Skillet with Quick-Fried Egg (page 89) (leftovers)	Baked Salmon with Greek Veggies & Avocado Tzatziki (page 118) (leftovers)
S	Raspberry-Lemon Baked Oatmeal Muffins (page 58) (leftovers)	Crispy Chickpea–Stuffed Sweet Potatoes (page 81) (leftovers)	Slow Cooker Red Curry (page 88)
S	Chai-Spiced Smoothie (page 50)	Heartland Harvest Tuna Melts (page 108)	Slow Cooker Red Curry (page 88) (leftovers)

	SNACKS	SIDES
+	Edamame-Avocado Hummus (page 133), Slathered Apple Snackers (page 131), Curry Tuna Salad Snackers (page 132) (to be eaten throughout the week)	Spiced Tabbouleh with Chickpeas (page 124) (can be made in a larger batch and enjoyed throughout the week)

PREP IT

Crispy Chickpea–Stuffed Sweet Potatoes (page 81): Prep and bake the sweet potatoes, then store until needed. Reheat in oven or microwave before stuffing and serving.

Spiced Tabbouleh with Chickpeas (page 124): Can be prepped on Sunday evening with leftover vegetables or herbs added throughout the week.

Raspberry-Lemon Baked Oatmeal Muffins (page 58): Bake, then store any unused muffins in the freezer until needed. Transfer to the refrigerator the night before to allow for thawing, then reheat in the microwave and pair with other preferred breakfast items.

Edamame-Avocado Hummus (page 133): Prep and store in the refrigerator until needed.

Chai-Spiced Smoothie (page 50): Brew tea bags and pour tea into ice molds for smoothies. Prepare additional tea throughout the week as a beverage option if desired.

SHOPPING LIST

Vegetables

- Avocados (2)
- Beans, green (½ pound)
- Bell pepper, red (1)
- Cabbage, shredded (1 bag, or use leftovers from Week 1)
- Carrots, large (2)
- Carrots, shredded (1 bag, or use leftovers from Week 1)
- Celery (1 bunch)
- Cilantro, fresh (1 bunch)
- Corn, sweet kernels, frozen (1 bag) or 1 can
- Cucumbers (4)
- Garlic (1 head or jar)
- Kale, green (1 or 2 bunches)
- Leafy greens or spring mix (1 large container)
- Mint, fresh (1 bunch)
- Onion, yellow (1)
- Onions, red (2)
- Parsley, fresh (1 bunch)
- Potatoes, sweet (5 large)
- Scallions (1 bunch)
- Spinach, baby (1 bag)
- Tomatoes, cherry (1 container)
- Tomatoes, Roma (2)
- Tomatoes, sun-dried (1 bag)

Fruit

- ⁎ Apples, Granny Smith
- ⁎ Apricots, dried (¼ cup)
- ⁎ Bananas (1 or 2)
- ⁎ Blueberries, frozen (1 bag)
- ⁎ Lemons (2 or 3)
- ⁎ Limes (1 or 2)
- ⁎ Peaches, frozen (1 bag)
- ⁎ Raspberries (2 pints)

Beans & Legumes

- ⁎ Beans, black, 1 (15.5-ounce) can
- ⁎ Beans, cannellini or great northern, 1 (15.5-ounce) can
- ⁎ Chickpeas, 2 (14.5-ounce) cans
- ⁎ Edamame, frozen, shelled (1 bag, or use leftovers from Week 1)
- ⁎ Hummus (1 container)
- ⁎ Tempeh, 1 (8-ounce) package
- ⁎ Tofu, firm, 2 (14-ounce) packages

Whole Grains

- ⁎ Bread, whole-wheat (1 loaf)
- ⁎ Bulgur, uncooked (½ cup)
- ⁎ Oats, rolled, uncooked (3½ cups)
- ⁎ Rice, brown, uncooked (3 cups)

Seafood

- ⁎ Salmon, fresh or frozen, 4 (6-ounce) fillets
- ⁎ Tuna, white, packed in water, 3 (5-ounce) cans

Nuts & Seeds

- ⁎ Almonds, slivered (¾ cup)
- ⁎ Pistachios, shelled (¼ cup)
- ⁎ Sunflower seeds, roasted (½ cup)
- ⁎ Tahini (1 jar)

Dairy & Eggs

- Cheese, Cheddar, sliced (1 package)
- Cheese, cottage, low-fat (1 container)
- Cheese, feta, crumbled (1 package, or use leftovers from Week 1)
- Eggs, large (1 dozen)
- Kefir, plain or vanilla (1 bottle)
- Yogurt, Greek, plain, low-fat (2 containers)

Other Items

- Chipotles in adobo sauce, 1 (7-ounce) can
- Coconut milk, 1 (13-ounce) can
- Tea, chai (1 box)

WEEK 3 SUGGESTED MEAL PLAN

	BREAKFAST	LUNCH	DINNER
M	Peaches & Cream Overnight Oats (page 56) (prep Sunday night)	Slow Cooker Red Curry (page 88) (leftovers)	Salmon Burgers with Crunchy Cabbage Slaw (page 103)
T	Peaches & Cream Overnight Oats (page 56) (leftovers)	Salmon Burgers with Crunchy Cabbage Slaw (page 103) (leftovers)	Shrimp Fried Rice–Style Freekeh (page 100)
W	Caprese-Style Avocado Toast (page 54)	Shrimp Fried Rice–Style Freekeh (page 100) (leftovers)	Salmon Burgers with Crunchy Cabbage Slaw (page 103) (leftovers)
T	Ginger-Berry Smoothie (page 51)	Shrimp Fried Rice–Style Freekeh (page 100) (leftovers)	Gouda Tuna Noodle Casserole (page 120)
F	Toasted Coconut Breakfast Bowls (page 52) (prep Thursday night)	Gouda Tuna Noodle Casserole (page 120) (leftovers)	Shrimp & Scallop Skewers with Chimichurri Sauce (page 109)
S	Toasted Coconut Breakfast Bowls (page 52) (leftovers)	Grown-Up Grilled Cheese with Sun-Dried Tomatoes (page 92)	Shrimp Fried Rice–Style Freekeh (page 100) (leftovers)
S	Caprese-Style Avocado Toast (page 54)	Gouda Tuna Noodle Casserole (page 120) (leftovers)	Grilled Swordfish with Chimichurri & Roasted Vegetables (page 98)

	SNACKS	SIDES
+	Smoky Sweet Potato Dip (page 136), Smoked Salmon Deviled Eggs (page 134) (to be eaten throughout the week)	Confetti Quinoa with Honey-Lime Dressing (page 130) (can be made in a larger batch and enjoyed throughout the week)

PREP IT

Peaches & Cream Overnight Oats (page 56): Prepare Sunday night and seal. Chill until ready to serve.

Confetti Quinoa with Honey-Lime Dressing (page 130): Prep on Sunday night and portion into multiple servings, or leave as a mixed quinoa salad and add leftover vegetables and herbs throughout the week.

Smoky Sweet Potato Dip (page 136): Prep on Sunday night and chill until ready to serve.

Toasted Coconut Breakfast Bowls (page 52): Batch cook quinoa while preparing the Confetti Quinoa with Honey-Lime Dressing (page 130) and chill until needed. Assemble on Thursday night to serve later in the week.

SHOPPING LIST

Vegetables

- Avocados (2)
- Basil, fresh (1 bunch)
- Bell pepper, green (1)
- Bell pepper, orange (1)
- Bell pepper, red (1)
- Cabbage, shredded (1 bag, or use leftovers from Week 2)
- Carrot (1 large)
- Carrots, shredded (1 bag, or use leftovers from Week 2)
- Cauliflower (1 small head)
- Cilantro, fresh (1 bunch)
- Corn, frozen, kernels (1 bag, or use leftovers from Week 2)
- Garlic (1 head or 1 jar)
- Leafy greens or spring mix (1 large container)
- Mushrooms, white or baby bella (8 ounces)
- Onions, red (3)
- Onions, yellow (2)
- Oregano, fresh (1 bunch)
- Parsley, fresh (1 bunch)
- Potatoes, sweet (2 large)
- Scallions (1 bunch)
- Spinach (1 bag)
- Tomatoes, cherry (1 container)
- Tomatoes, sun-dried (1 bag, or use leftovers from Week 2)
- Zucchini (1 large)

Fruit

- Bananas (1 or 2)
- Blueberries, frozen (1 bag, or use leftovers from Week 2)
- Lemons (2 or 3)
- Limes (1 or 2)
- Mango, fresh (1) or frozen (1 bag)
- Peaches (1 or 2)
- Peaches, frozen (1 bag, or use leftovers from Week 2)
- Strawberries (1 pint)

Beans & Legumes

- Chickpeas, 1 (14.5-ounce) can
- Peas, frozen (1 bag)

Whole Grains

- Beans, black, 1 (15.5-ounce) can
- English muffins, whole-grain if available (1 package)
- Freekeh, uncooked (1½ cups)
- Oats, rolled, uncooked (2½ cups)
- Pasta, whole-grain, rotini (1 box)
- Quinoa, uncooked (2 cups)

Seafood

- Salmon, 2 (6-ounce) cans
- Salmon, smoked (2 ounces)
- Scallops, sea (¾ pound medium)
- Shrimp, fresh or frozen, peeled and deveined (1¾ pounds)
- Swordfish, 4 (6-ounce) steaks
- Tuna, white, packed in water, 2 (5-ounce) cans

Nuts & Seeds

* Almonds, slivered (¾ cup)
* Hemp hearts (1 bag, or use leftovers from Week 1)
* Pecans, chopped (¼ cup)
* Tahini (or use what was purchased in Week 2)

Eggs & Dairy

* Cheese, cottage, low-fat (1 container)
* Cheese, Gouda, shredded (1 package)
* Cheese, Havarti or mozzarella, sliced (1 package)
* Cheese, mozzarella, fresh, pearls (1 container)
* Cream cheese, low-fat (1 block, or use leftovers from Week 2)
* Kefir, plain or vanilla (1 bottle)

Other Items

* Coconut milk, 1 (13-ounce) can
* Coconut, unsweetened flakes (1 bag, or use leftovers from Week 1)

Zucchini Pancakes with Smoked Salmon, page 55

— 4 —
BREAKFASTS

CHAI-SPICED SMOOTHIE

Serves 1

PREP TIME: 5 minutes, plus overnight to freeze

QUICK PREP GLUTEN-FREE VEGETARIAN

Elevate your morning smoothie to something more filling and satisfying than a fruit and yogurt mix. The oats and banana boost the prebiotic fiber, and when combined with the probiotics found in kefir, you have a winning combination for gut health and great flavor. You can also use the premade chai tea ice cubes to flavor iced coffee during hot summer months. Make sure to check your oats are gluten-free if that's a concern for you.

4 fluid ounces water

1 chai tea bag

¼ cup uncooked rolled oats

½ cup plain, low-fat kefir

1 banana, sliced (about ¾ cup)

½ tablespoon hemp hearts, plus more for garnish

1 teaspoon honey

Dash ground cinnamon, plus more for garnish

1. In a kettle or a small saucepan, heat the water until boiling. Remove from the heat and pour into a mug. Add the tea bag and steep for about 5 minutes. Cool, pour the tea into an ice cube tray (about 4 cubes), and freeze overnight.

2. When ready to prepare the smoothie, in your blender, combine the oats, kefir, banana, hemp hearts, honey, and cinnamon. Add the chai tea ice cubes to the blender.

3. Blend on high speed for 30 to 60 seconds, stopping and scraping the sides of the blender with a spatula if needed, until the texture becomes smooth and creamy.

4. Pour the smoothie into a tall glass. Garnish with a sprinkle of cinnamon or additional hemp hearts, if desired, and serve immediately.

VARIATION: Any variety of chai tea will work for this recipe, so find a brand and flavor that fits your taste preferences. For a milder flavor, brew for half the time.

PER SERVING:

Calories: 310; Total Fat: 11g; Saturated Fat: 4g; Polyunsaturated Fat: 1g; Monounsaturated Fat: 1.5g; Cholesterol: 5mg; Sodium: 65mg; Carbohydrates: 54g; Fiber: 6g; Sugars: 26g; Added Sugars: 5.5g; Protein: 13g

GINGER-BERRY SMOOTHIE

Serves 1

PREP TIME: 5 minutes

QUICK PREP GLUTEN-FREE VEGETARIAN

Frozen fruit is a staple in my freezer so I can whip up a quick smoothie anytime. I use low-fat cottage cheese for protein in smoothies because it's low-cost and convenient to use. Trust me, you don't notice anything but the fruity flavors in this delicious smoothie.

1 cup frozen blueberries

½ cup frozen peaches

1½ cups loosely packed fresh spinach

½ cup 2% milk cottage cheese

¾ cup plain, low-fat kefir

1 teaspoon honey

1 teaspoon ground ginger

1. In your blender, combine the blueberries, peaches, spinach, cottage cheese, kefir, honey and ginger. Blend on high for 30 to 60 seconds, until the texture becomes creamy and smooth. Pause to scrape the sides of the blender with a spatula if needed.

2. If the texture is too thick, add water 1 tablespoon at a time until desired consistency is reached. Pour the smoothie into a tall glass and serve immediately.

VARIATION: Add some extra zest to this smoothie by using fresh ginger root or crystallized ginger in place of ground ginger. Adjust the flavor to your preference by adding more or less than 1 teaspoon.

PER SERVING:

Calories: 320; Total Fat: 12g; Saturated Fat: 2.5g; Polyunsaturated Fat: 1g; Monounsaturated Fat: 1g; Cholesterol: 20mg; Sodium: 500mg; Carbohydrates: 48g; Fiber: 7g; Sugars: 39g; Added Sugars: 5.5g; Protein: 24g

TOASTED COCONUT
BREAKFAST BOWLS

Serves 4

PREP TIME: 5 minutes / COOK TIME: 25 minutes

30 MINUTES GLUTEN-FREE VEGETARIAN

I've always loved oatmeal, but I don't feel fully satisfied unless I add enough fat and protein. This version offers a balanced breakfast that can be enjoyed hot or chilled when prepped in advance. Add your favorite nuts, seeds, or spices on top to make it your own. Make sure to check your oats are gluten-free if that's a concern for you.

1 cup canned coconut milk

1¼ cups water

½ cup uncooked quinoa

⅛ teaspoon salt

1½ cups uncooked rolled oats

1 teaspoon vanilla extract

½ teaspoon ground cinnamon

½ teaspoon ground cardamom

½ cup unsweetened coconut flakes

½ cup sliced or slivered almonds

1 large banana, peeled and sliced

1. In a medium saucepan over high heat, bring the coconut milk and water to a boil. Add the quinoa and salt, then reduce the heat to a simmer. Cook for 15 minutes, or until the quinoa is fully cooked. Add the oats, vanilla, cinnamon, and cardamom. Cook for several minutes more, until the oats are softened and most of the liquid is absorbed.

2. Meanwhile, heat a small nonstick skillet over medium-low heat. Add the coconut flakes and almonds, and gently toast, stirring, until they become fragrant and begin to brown, about 5 minutes. Remove from the heat and immediately transfer out of the hot skillet into a small bowl to avoid burning.

3. To serve, spoon the quinoa-oat mixture into four bowls. Top with one quarter of the toasted almonds and coconut flakes. Distribute the banana among the bowls and serve immediately.

VARIATION: Recreate this bowl with other grains such as freekeh or sorghum in place of quinoa. Prepped bowls may be refrigerated for up to 5 days and enjoyed chilled or reheated in the microwave in 20-second increments.

PER SERVING:

Calories: 470; Total Fat: 27g; Saturated Fat: 16g; Polyunsaturated Fat: 3.5g; Monounsaturated Fat: 6g; Cholesterol: 0mg; Sodium: 105mg; Carbohydrates: 49g; Fiber: 9g; Sugars: 7g; Added Sugars: 0g; Protein: 12g

BREAKFAST MASON JARS

Serves 4

PREP TIME: 5 minutes / COOK TIME: 25 minutes

30 MINUTES GLUTEN-FREE VEGETARIAN

A savory, filling breakfast helps me start my day on the right foot. This flexible meal-prep recipe can include your favorite seasonal produce or use scrambled eggs instead of tofu.

2½ cups low-sodium vegetable stock

1¼ cup dry green split peas

1 (14-ounce) block firm tofu

2 tablespoons chopped chipotles in adobo sauce

½ cup shredded pepper Jack cheese

1½ cups fresh spinach

1 cup halved cherry tomatoes

1 avocado, diced

1. In a small saucepan over high heat, bring the stock to a boil. Add the dry green split peas and reduce to a simmer. Cook for 15 to 20 minutes, or until all liquid is absorbed. Remove from the heat and allow to cool.

2. While the split peas are cooking, drain and press the block of tofu to remove excess liquid. Heat a large skillet over medium-high heat. Add the block of tofu and break apart with a spatula as if browning ground beef. Add the chipotles in adobo sauce, and stir to combine. Cook, stirring, for 10 minutes, or until the mixture is dry and crumbly.

3. Evenly divide the cooked split peas into each of four mason jars or food-storage containers. Add one quarter of the spicy tofu mixture on top of each. Layer in the remaining ingredients in the following order: cheese, spinach, tomatoes, and avocado.

4. Allow to cool completely if not serving immediately. Store in the refrigerator up to 5 days. Reheat by transferring to a microwave-safe bowl and heating in 30-second increments.

INGREDIENT TIP: Use canned or precooked lentils to shorten your prep time. Wait to add the diced avocado until serving to minimize excessive browning.

PER SERVING:

Calories: 260; Total Fat: 8g; Saturated Fat: 2g; Polyunsaturated Fat: 1g; Monounsaturated Fat: 4g; Cholesterol: 10mg; Sodium: 340mg; Carbohydrates: 41g; Fiber: 18g; Sugars: 5g; Added Sugars: 0g; Protein: 19g

CAPRESE-STYLE AVOCADO TOAST

Serves 1

PREP TIME: 10 minutes

QUICK PREP VEGETARIAN

This super speedy breakfast combines my love of caprese salad and avocado toast. I like to serve mine open faced, but it can also be made into a breakfast sandwich. Just be careful; it can get a little messy.

1 whole-wheat English muffin, halved

½ ripe avocado, cut into ¼-inch cubes

3 or 4 fresh basil leaves, chopped or torn

½ cup halved cherry tomatoes

1 ounce fresh mozzarella pearls, halved

2 teaspoons balsamic glaze

1. Lightly toast the English muffin.

2. Use a spoon to gently scoop the avocado onto the two halves of the English muffin, and mash it with the back of the spoon.

3. Layer the fresh basil on top of the avocado. Arrange the cherry tomatoes and mozzarella pearls, flat-side down, on top of the basil. Drizzle each half with the balsamic glaze and serve immediately.

LEFTOVERS: Repeat for an afternoon snack to avoid wasting the other half of the avocado, or add it to one of your lunch or dinner meals.

PER SERVING:

Calories: 350; Total Fat: 16g; Saturated Fat: 4.5g; Polyunsaturated Fat: 2g; Monounsaturated Fat: 8.5g; Cholesterol: 20mg; Sodium: 420mg; Carbohydrates: 39g; Fiber: 10g; Sugars: 10g; Added Sugars: 0g; Protein: 15g

ZUCCHINI PANCAKES WITH SMOKED SALMON

Serves 4

PREP TIME: 10 minutes / COOK TIME: 20 minutes

30 MINUTES

Enjoy these savory pancakes for breakfast or brunch on the weekends, or batch cook them for easy reheating during the week. You will find that zucchini peaks during summer months, but shredded zucchini can be frozen and stored so you can repeat this recipe year-round.

**2 cups tightly packed
shredded zucchini**

½ red onion, diced (about ½ cup)

½ cup shredded pepper Jack cheese

2 garlic cloves, minced

½ teaspoon dried basil

4 large eggs, lightly beaten

¾ cup all-purpose flour

½ teaspoon baking soda

4 tablespoons low-fat cream cheese

4 ounces smoked salmon

1. Squeeze the shredded zucchini tightly over a colander or fine-mesh strainer to remove excess liquid.

2. Heat a large skillet over medium to medium-high heat. In a large mixing bowl, stir together the zucchini, onion, pepper Jack cheese, garlic, basil, eggs, flour, and baking soda until a batter forms.

3. Drop the batter into the heated skillet to form 5- to 6-inch pancakes (about ⅓ cup of batter). Cook for 2 to 3 minutes on one side, then flip and cook for 2 to 3 minutes more. The pancake should brown slightly on each side. Repeat with the remaining batter to make eight pancakes total.

4. To serve, spread cream cheese on top of each pancake and top with smoked salmon. Serve immediately.

LEFTOVERS: If batch cooking for meal planning, allow the pancakes to cool completely before storing in the fridge. Stack pancakes with wax paper between layers. To reheat, transfer to a skillet and warm over low heat or microwave in 20-second increments until pancakes are warm.

PER SERVING (2 PANCAKES):

Calories: 310; Total Fat: 11g; Saturated Fat: 5g; Polyunsaturated Fat: 2g; Monounsaturated Fat: 4g; Cholesterol: 210mg; Sodium: 640mg; Carbohydrates: 33g; Fiber: 3g; Sugars: 5g; Added Sugars: 0g; Protein: 21g

PEACHES & CREAM OVERNIGHT OATS

Serves 2

PREP TIME: 5 minutes, plus overnight to chill

QUICK PREP GLUTEN-FREE VEGETARIAN

Overnight oats are a year-round staple in our house because they can be enjoyed straight from the fridge when it's hot or warmed in the microwave when it's cold. This version can be made with fresh or frozen peaches, and you get a gut-friendly boost by using kefir. Be sure to look for gluten-free oats if that's a concern for you.

1 cup uncooked rolled oats

1½ cups plain, low-fat kefir

¼ cup chopped pecans

2 tablespoons hemp hearts

1 teaspoon ground cinnamon

½ teaspoon vanilla extract

1½ cups diced peaches

2 teaspoons honey

1. Divide the oats, kefir, pecans, hemp hearts, cinnamon, and vanilla between two mason jars or food storage containers. Stir gently to combine, then top with the diced peaches.

2. Seal and refrigerate to chill overnight. When ready to serve, remove the lids and drizzle the honey over the top. Stir to combine before eating.

INGREDIENT TIP: If using frozen peaches, allow to thaw slightly for easier dicing. They can remain partially frozen as they will have time to fully thaw overnight. If you prefer a crunchier texture, reserve the chopped pecans and add in the morning.

PER SERVING:

Calories: 440; Total Fat: 25g; Saturated Fat: 3g; Polyunsaturated Fat: 7.5g; Monounsaturated Fat: 7g; Cholesterol: 10mg; Sodium: 95mg; Carbohydrates: 54g; Fiber: 9g; Sugars: 23g; Added Sugars: 3g; Protein: 19g

HEARTY HASH BROWN
BREAKFAST BOWLS

Serves 4

PREP TIME: 5 minutes / COOK TIME: 20 minutes

30 MINUTES GLUTEN-FREE VEGETARIAN

Potatoes are one of my favorite ingredients because they're versatile, affordable, and work well with many flavors. This breakfast bowl can be prepped ahead for reheated breakfasts or served up hot and fresh on mornings when you have more time to cook.

1 (15.5-ounce) can black beans, drained and rinsed

1 tablespoon canola oil

4 cups shredded potatoes or frozen hash browns (gluten-free if needed)

1 white or yellow onion, diced

1 red bell pepper, diced

1 cup sliced white mushrooms

4 large eggs

⅔ cup salsa or pico de gallo

1 avocado, diced

Pinch salt

Pinch freshly ground black pepper

Fresh cilantro, for garnish

1. Drain and rinse the black beans and set aside. In a large skillet over medium-high heat, heat the canola oil while you prep the vegetables.

2. Add the potatoes, onion, and red bell pepper. Cook for 10 minutes, flipping occasionally, or until the potatoes begin to brown and crisp. Add the mushrooms

and cook for 3 to 5 minutes more, until browned and tender. Transfer to bowls or food storage containers, dividing evenly into four servings.

3. In the same skillet, fry or scramble the eggs. Add one cooked egg to each bowl. Top with a quarter each of the black beans, salsa, and avocado. Season with salt and pepper to taste. Garnish with fresh cilantro, if using, and serve or refrigerate.

VARIATION: Replace the shredded hash brown potatoes with spiralized sweet potatoes, cubed or diced potatoes, or thinly sliced potatoes. Adjust cooking time accordingly to achieve your preferred level of crispiness.

PER SERVING:

Calories: 450; Total Fat: 15g; Saturated Fat: 3g; Polyunsaturated Fat: 3.5g; Monounsaturated Fat: 7.5g; Cholesterol: 185mg; Sodium: 470mg; Carbohydrates: 64g; Fiber: 13g; Sugars: 8g; Added Sugars: 0g; Protein: 18g

RASPBERRY-LEMON BAKED OATMEAL MUFFINS

Makes 12 muffins

PREP TIME: 10 minutes / COOK TIME: 30 minutes

GLUTEN-FREE VEGETARIAN

Baked oatmeal is a great option for meal prep but not always the most convenient to take with you. I created this on-the-go version so you can head out the door with a one-handed breakfast. You can top it with peanut or almond butter. You can pair it with a piece of fresh fruit or a hard-boiled egg, if you prefer a heartier breakfast.

3 cups uncooked rolled oats

⅓ cup sugar

1½ teaspoons baking powder

1 teaspoon ground cinnamon

½ teaspoon salt

1 tablespoon lemon zest

2 large eggs, lightly beaten

2½ cups 2% milk

1 teaspoon vanilla extract

1¾ cups fresh raspberries

¾ cup slivered almonds

1. Preheat the oven to 350°F. Line a muffin tin with cup liners.

2. In a large mixing bowl, fold to combine the oats, sugar, baking powder, cinnamon, salt, and lemon zest. In another large mixing bowl, stir to combine the eggs, milk, and vanilla extract, then add to the dry ingredients. Stir to combine, then add the raspberries and almonds. Do not overmix. The mixture will be very wet with excess liquid.

3. Spoon the mixture into the muffin tin, dividing evenly. Bake for 30 minutes, or until the muffins are set and the tops begin to brown.

4. Remove from the oven and allow to cool slightly before serving.

SERVING SUGGESTION: To enjoy immediately, break the muffin apart in a bowl and top with Greek yogurt, fresh berries, or additional almonds. To store, place the muffins in a sealed zip-top bag or airtight food storage container. Store for up to one week.

PER SERVING (1 MUFFIN):

Calories: 220; Total Fat: 8g; Saturated Fat: 1.5g; Polyunsaturated Fat: 1.5g; Monounsaturated Fat: 3.5g; Cholesterol: 35mg; Sodium: 135mg; Carbohydrates: 29g; Fiber: 5g; Sugars: 10g; Added Sugars: 5.5g; Protein: 8g

SAVORY POTATO FRITTATA WITH SMOKED TROUT

Serves 6

PREP TIME: 10 minutes / COOK TIME: 30 minutes

GLUTEN-FREE

Frittatas are a convenient make-ahead breakfast for weekend brunches or weekday mornings. I like to serve mine with barely dressed greens or toast to complete the meal.

2 yellow potatoes, peeled and cut into 3- to 4-inch pieces

1½ cups chopped asparagus (1-inch pieces)

1 tablespoon extra-virgin olive oil, divided

8 large eggs

1½ tablespoons 2% milk

Pinch salt

Pinch freshly ground black pepper

8 ounces smoked trout

1 tablespoon chopped fresh dill, divided

¼ cup feta cheese

4 cups loosely packed mixed salad greens

Freshly squeezed lemon juice (optional)

1. Preheat the oven to 450°F.

2. Bring a large saucepan of water to a boil and cook the potatoes for 10 minutes, or until tender. Place in a colander. Add the asparagus to the pot and boil for about 1 minute, or until crisp-tender, then transfer with a slotted spoon to the colander. Rinse the potatoes and asparagus under cold water to cool.

3. Add ½ tablespoon of oil to a large cast iron or oven-safe skillet. Coat the surface and heat over medium-high heat. Meanwhile, in a large mixing bowl, whisk the eggs and milk together. Season with salt and pepper.

4. Cut the potatoes into thin slices. Flake the smoked trout with a fork, then layer in the skillet along with the potatoes and asparagus. Pour the egg mixture on top. Sprinkle ½ tablespoon of dill on top, along with the feta cheese.

5. Cook for 7 to 8 minutes on the stove top, or until the frittata is set along the edges and wobbly in the middle.

6. Transfer the skillet to the preheated oven and bake for 5 to 8 minutes more, or until the edges begin to brown and pull away from the pan. Remove, then cut into six wedges. Lightly dress the salad greens with the remaining ½ tablespoon of olive oil and the lemon juice, if using. Garnish with the remaining ½ tablespoon of dill, and serve immediately. Store leftovers, refrigerated, for up to 4 days.

continued

Savory Potato Frittata with Smoked Trout *continued*

VARIATION: If you don't have a cast iron or oven-safe skillet, skip the stove-top cooking. Preheat the oven to 375°F. Layer the ingredients in a square baking pan, then pour the egg mixture over the top. Reduce the oven temperature to 375°F and bake until fully set in the center.

PER SERVING:

Calories: 310; Total Fat: 15g; Saturated Fat: 4g; Polyunsaturated Fat: 2.5g; Monounsaturated Fat: 7g; Cholesterol: 280mg; Sodium: 290mg; Carbohydrates: 22g; Fiber: 3g; Sugars: 2g; Added Sugars: 0g; Protein: 23g

Seafood Gumbo-Laya, page 76

SOUPS & SALADS

Spring Greens Panzanella Salad with Shrimp, 64

Sea Breeze Salmon Salad with Margarita Dressing, 65

Massaged Kale Salad with Sesame-Lime Dressing, 66

Green Bean Niçoise Salad with Tuna, 67

Citrus Caprese Salad, 69

Crunchy Cruciferous Caesar Salad, 70

Creamy Cauliflower Soup with Spiced Chickpeas, 71

Smoked Oyster & Clam Chowder, 73

Fisherman's Stew in the Slow Cooker, 74

Vegetarian Chili with Butternut Squash, 75

Seafood Gumbo-Laya, 76

Creamy Crawfish Bisque, 77

SPRING GREENS PANZANELLA SALAD WITH SHRIMP

Serves 4

PREP TIME: 5 minutes / COOK TIME: 20 minutes

`30 MINUTES`

This salad always makes me want to dine alfresco. When grilling isn't an option, I reach for precooked frozen shrimp that I can quickly thaw and toss on top. When prepping lunches for the week, to keep everything fresh I store ingredients separately and wait to assemble until ready to eat.

½ pound precooked frozen shrimp

3 slices day-old French or sourdough bread, cut into bite-size cubes

10 medium asparagus spears

6 cups loosely packed fresh spinach

4 Roma tomatoes, quartered or sliced

½ red onion, thinly sliced

4 tablespoons extra-virgin olive oil

2 tablespoons balsamic vinegar

Pinch salt

1 avocado, diced

About 5 large fresh basil leaves

½ cup shredded Parmesan cheese

1. Thaw the shrimp by placing in a large bowl of cold water. Preheat the oven to 300°F.

2. Arrange the bread on a baking sheet in a single layer, and toast until it becomes crunchy, 5 to 10 minutes total, flipping once during baking.

3. Meanwhile, on a second baking sheet, arrange the asparagus in a single layer. After removing the bread, raise the oven temperature to 375°F and roast the asparagus until it's a vibrant green color and is cooked through, about 10 minutes.

4. In a salad bowl toss the spinach with the tomatoes, onion, olive oil, vinegar, and salt.

5. Add the avocado to the salad. Once the asparagus is roasted, cut into 1- to 2-inch pieces and add to the bowl. Mix to combine, then peel the shrimp and add to the salad. Top with the toasted bread. Toss one last time, then transfer to four bowls or plates. Chiffonade the basil (see tip), garnish with the basil and Parmesan cheese, and serve.

INGREDIENT TIP: Here is how to chiffonade basil: First, wash the leaves and dry thoroughly. Stack them in one pile, then tightly roll lengthwise. Using a chef's knife, thinly slice the leaves, cutting perpendicular to the stem. The result should be thin ribbons of basil to use as a garnish or mix into your salad.

PER SERVING:

Calories: 530; Total Fat: 23g; Saturated Fat: 4.5g; Polyunsaturated Fat: 3g; Monounsaturated Fat: 14.5g; Cholesterol: 125mg; Sodium: 1,080mg; Carbohydrates: 55g; Fiber: 7g; Sugars: 8g; Added Sugars: 0g; Protein: 28g

SEA BREEZE SALMON SALAD WITH MARGARITA DRESSING

Serves 4

PREP TIME: 5 minutes / COOK TIME: 15 minutes

30 MINUTES GLUTEN-FREE

This summertime salad recipe brings island flavors to your table. Fresh fruit and a sweet lime dressing complement the salmon flavored with Jamaican jerk seasoning.

1 pound fresh or frozen salmon fillets, cut into 4 pieces

5 tablespoons extra-virgin olive oil, divided

3 tablespoons freshly squeezed lime juice, divided

2 teaspoons Jamaican jerk seasoning

6 cups tightly packed mixed greens or spring mix lettuce

1 cup fresh strawberries, sliced

1 mango, diced

1 avocado, diced

¼ cup sliced or slivered almonds

1 tablespoon honey

1½ teaspoons ground cumin

⅛ teaspoon salt

Fresh cilantro, for garnish

1. Thaw the fish in cold water if using frozen, and preheat the oven to 400°F.

2. Place the fillets on a baking sheet, and brush with 1 tablespoon of olive oil, then drizzle with 1 tablespoon of lime juice and sprinkle with the jerk seasoning. Broil the fish on the top rack for 12 to 14 minutes, or until it reaches an internal temperature of 145°F and the salmon flakes easily with a fork. Remove from the oven and allow to cool.

3. Meanwhile, in a large serving bowl, layer the salad greens followed by the strawberries, mango, avocado, and almonds. Toss gently to mix.

4. In a small bowl, prepare the dressing by whisking together the remaining 4 tablespoons of olive oil, the remaining 2 tablespoons of lime juice, and the honey, cumin, and salt.

5. To serve, arrange the salad mix on 4 plates. Top each salad with one salmon fillet, and gently flake apart. Add the dressing, and garnish with fresh cilantro, if desired.

INGREDIENT TIP: If you're short on time, skip the baking step and use canned salmon instead. Distribute over the top of the salad and sprinkle with jerk seasoning before adding the dressing.

PER SERVING:

Calories: 570; Total Fat: 41g; Saturated Fat: 5g; Polyunsaturated Fat: 7.5g; Monounsaturated Fat: 22g; Cholesterol: 60mg; Sodium: 380mg; Carbohydrates: 28g; Fiber: 6g; Sugars: 19g; Added Sugars: 4.5g; Protein: 27g

MASSAGED KALE SALAD WITH SESAME-LIME DRESSING

Serves 4

PREP TIME: 10 minutes

QUICK PREP GLUTEN-FREE VEGETARIAN

This side salad is quick and easy to make! It's delicious and healthy to boot. And you get to play with your food. Turn this side salad into a pescatarian diet–friendly entrée by topping it with your favorite protein, such as seared tofu, grilled shrimp, or baked salmon.

6 cups fresh kale, tightly packed

1½ tablespoons sesame oil

¼ teaspoon coarse sea salt

Juice of 1 lime

1 teaspoon honey

1½ cups shredded red cabbage

1 cup shelled edamame

½ cup slivered or sliced almonds

1. Wash and dry the kale, stripping from stems if necessary. Chop or tear into bite-size pieces before measuring into a large mixing bowl.

2. Add the sesame oil and sea salt. Use clean, dry hands to massage the kale, working it between your fingers. Continue for 2 to 3 minutes, or until the kale is reduced to about half its original volume and becomes a deep green color.

3. In a small bowl, combine the lime juice and honey, and drizzle over the kale. Add the red cabbage, edamame, and almonds to the large mixing bowl, and toss to combine. Serve immediately or chill in the refrigerator for up to 30 minutes first.

INGREDIENT TIP: Coarse sea salt is vital for this recipe. The coarser texture will help break down the fibrous kale for a more tender salad.

PER SERVING:

Calories: 250; Total Fat: 17g; Saturated Fat: 2g; Polyunsaturated Fat: 5.5g; Monounsaturated Fat: 8.5g; Cholesterol: 0mg; Sodium: 190mg; Carbohydrates: 19g; Fiber: 8g; Sugars: 6g; Added Sugars: 1.5g; Protein: 12g

GREEN BEAN NIÇOISE SALAD WITH TUNA

Serves 4

PREP TIME: 10 minutes / COOK TIME: 30 minutes

GLUTEN-FREE

This updated version of the classic French salad is an easy way to upgrade your midweek salads. Prep the potatoes, green beans, and hard-boiled eggs in advance to reduce prep time and enjoy leftovers throughout the week.

8 ounces small new potatoes

1 pound fresh green beans, trimmed

4 large eggs

¼ cup extra-virgin olive oil

½ red onion, finely chopped

1½ tablespoons freshly squeezed lemon juice

2 teaspoons Dijon mustard

1 teaspoon honey

1 tablespoon chopped fresh dill, plus more for garnish

Pinch salt

Pinch freshly ground black pepper

¼ cup Kalamata or Niçoise olives, pitted and halved

1 small bunch radishes, about 6 to 8 total, trimmed and quartered

2 cans tuna packed in water, drained

2 tablespoons capers, drained (optional)

1. Scrub the potatoes and place in a medium saucepan. Cover with water and bring to a boil. Cook until the potatoes are tender when pierced with a fork, 12 to 15 minutes. Prepare a large bowl of ice water, and transfer the cooked potatoes to the ice bath. Chill for 3 minutes, then remove and dry with a paper towel. Set aside.

2. Meanwhile, blanch the green beans by bringing a large saucepan of water to a boil. Add the green beans and cook 2 to 4 minutes, or until crisp-tender. Transfer to the ice bath using tongs or a slotted spoon. Chill for 3 minutes, then remove and dry with a paper towel. Set aside.

3. Add the eggs to the same pot used for the green beans, and bring the water back to a boil. Boil the eggs for 8 to 10 minutes, then transfer to the ice bath. Refresh with more ice if needed. Chill until cold, about 5 minutes. Peel the eggs and set aside.

4. In a small bowl, prepare the dressing by whisking together the olive oil, onion, lemon juice, mustard, honey, dill, salt, and pepper.

continued

5. In a large bowl, toss the blanched green beans with about half of the dressing. Cut the cooled potatoes into large cubes and the eggs into whatever size you like; arrange on a serving platter, then top with the potatoes, eggs, olives, radishes, and tuna. Drizzle the remaining dressing over the salad, garnish with fresh dill and the capers (if using), and serve.

VARIATION: Replace the canned tuna with canned salmon, slices of seared tuna, or cooked shrimp.

PER SERVING:

Calories: 400; Total Fat: 22g; Saturated Fat: 4.5g; Polyunsaturated Fat: 3.5g; Monounsaturated Fat: 13g; Cholesterol: 220mg; Sodium: 610mg; Carbohydrates: 21g; Fiber: 5g; Sugars: 6g; Added Sugars: 1.5g; Protein: 30g

CITRUS CAPRESE SALAD

Serves 4

PREP TIME: 10 minutes

`QUICK PREP` `GLUTEN-FREE` `VEGETARIAN`

As much as I love a traditional caprese salad, it can be downright impossible to find fresh tomatoes year-round. This version opens the possibility to enjoy it no matter the weather by utilizing winter citrus fruits.

2 cups fresh spinach, washed and dried

2 cups fresh arugula, washed and dried

1 red grapefruit

1 blood orange

1 Valencia or navel orange

8 ounces fresh mozzarella

¼ cup fresh basil leaves, washed and dried (optional)

4 tablespoons extra-virgin olive oil

2 tablespoons balsamic glaze

Pinch salt

Pinch freshly ground black pepper

1. On a serving platter or in a large salad bowl, arrange the spinach and arugula.

2. Using a chef's knife, slice the top and bottom from the grapefruit so it sits flat on a cutting board. Use the chef's knife to carefully slice away the peel and pith, leaving the flesh of the grapefruit intact. Turn the peeled grapefruit on its side and thinly slice. Add the grapefruit slices to the fresh greens.

3. Repeat with the blood orange and the Valencia orange, layering the slices randomly on the platter or in the bowl.

4. Slice the ball of mozzarella into similarly sized slices and layer among the citrus.

5. Chiffonade 8 to 10 large leaves of the basil, if using, (see the Ingredient Tip on page 64) and add to the salad.

6. Drizzle with olive oil and balsamic glaze, and season with salt and pepper to taste. Serve immediately. If not serving right away, store prepped ingredients separately and do not dress the salad. Assemble upon serving to maintain freshness.

SUBSTITUTION: If fresh basil is not available, substitute additional spinach instead. You may also use balsamic vinegar instead of glaze for a less sweet dressing.

PER SERVING:

Calories: 270; Total Fat: 16g; Saturated Fat: 7g; Polyunsaturated Fat: 1g; Monounsaturated Fat: 7.5g; Cholesterol: 35mg; Sodium: 410mg; Carbohydrates: 18g; Fiber: 4g; Sugars: 11g; Added Sugars: 0g; Protein: 15g

CRUNCHY CRUCIFEROUS CAESAR SALAD

Serves 4

PREP TIME: 15 minutes

`30 MINUTES` `GLUTEN-FREE`

I've always been a fan of Caesar salads, but when I enjoyed them as a meal I was often left hungry and unsatisfied. This version pumps up the fiber with crunchy veggies. And with the option to add a protein, you can enjoy it as a side salad or a complete meal.

1 bunch curly green kale

12 large Brussels sprouts

1 cup shredded red or green cabbage

1 tablespoon extra-virgin olive oil

¼ cup slivered almonds

⅔ cup shaved Parmesan cheese, divided

1 cup mayonnaise

2 tablespoons freshly squeezed lemon juice

2 garlic cloves, finely minced

1½ teaspoons anchovy paste

1½ teaspoons Dijon mustard

1 teaspoon Worcestershire sauce

⅛ teaspoon freshly ground black pepper

1. Wash and dry the kale, Brussels sprouts, and cabbage. Strip the kale from the stems, and chop into bite-size pieces. Add the kale to a large mixing bowl, and drizzle with the olive oil. Use clean, dry hands to massage the kale, working it between your fingers until it reduces in volume and becomes a deep, vibrant green, 2 to 3 minutes.

2. Trim the stems from the Brussels sprouts, and remove any damaged outer leaves. Halve each Brussels sprout and place flat-side down on a cutting board. Use a chef's knife to slice as thin as possible. Repeat with the remaining Brussels sprouts and add to the kale.

3. Add the cabbage, almonds, and ⅓ cup of Parmesan cheese to the mixing bowl, and toss to combine.

4. In a small bowl, prepare the dressing by whisking the mayonnaise, lemon juice, garlic, anchovy paste, mustard, Worcestershire sauce, the remaining ⅓ cup of Parmesan cheese, and the black pepper together until well combined. Dress the salad to your preference, and toss to combine. Serve immediately.

INGREDIENT TIP: Speed up the prep time by using the slicing disk of your food processor for the Brussels sprouts or cabbage. You can also look for presliced options in the prepared foods section of your grocery store.

PER SERVING:

Calories: 440; Total Fat: 32g; Saturated Fat: 7g; Polyunsaturated Fat: 12.5g; Monounsaturated Fat: 11g; Cholesterol: 35mg; Sodium: 920mg; Carbohydrates: 30g; Fiber: 6g; Sugars: 8g; Added Sugars: 0g; Protein: 14g

CREAMY CAULIFLOWER SOUP WITH SPICED CHICKPEAS

Serves 4

PREP TIME: 10 minutes / COOK TIME: 30 minutes

GLUTEN-FREE VEGETARIAN

For most of my life I thought I didn't like the taste of cauliflower, but it was because I don't enjoy it when it is raw. Roasting it takes the flavor to a new level, and this creamy, blended soup is now a cold-weather favorite. If available, try adding za'atar seasoning as a garnish to really spice things up!

Nonstick cooking spray (optional)

1 large head cauliflower, cut into florets, with stalks, if desired

4 garlic cloves, minced

2 tablespoons extra-virgin olive oil, divided

Pinch salt

Pinch freshly ground black pepper

2 teaspoons ground cumin, divided

2 teaspoons red pepper flakes, divided, plus more for garnish

1 (14.5-ounce) can chickpeas, drained and rinsed

½ yellow onion, diced

3 cups low-sodium vegetable stock

1 (14-ounce) block silken tofu, drained

½ cup half-and-half

Fresh thyme, for garnish (optional)

1. Preheat the oven to 400°F. Line a baking sheet with parchment paper or spray with nonstick cooking spray.

2. Toss the cauliflower with the garlic, 1 tablespoon of olive oil, the salt and black pepper, and 1 teaspoon each of cumin and red pepper flakes. Arrange on the baking sheet in a single layer and bake on the upper or middle rack for 30 minutes, flipping once if desired for even browning.

3. Line a second baking sheet with parchment paper or spray with nonstick cooking spray. Dry the drained chickpeas, then toss with the remaining tablespoon of olive oil and the remaining teaspoon each of cumin and crushed red pepper. Arrange in a single layer. Add to the oven on the lower baking rack and roast for 20 minutes, or until crispy and toasted on the outside.

4. Meanwhile, add the onion to a large saucepan. Add the stock, and bring to a simmer.

5. When the cauliflower and chickpeas are finished, remove from the oven. Set the chickpeas aside along with a small reserve of roasted cauliflower florets for garnish. Add the remaining cauliflower and the silken tofu to the simmering stock. Reduce the heat, and stir to combine.

continued

6. Using an immersion blender, blend until a thick, creamy consistency is reached, about 2 minutes. Add the half-and-half, and blend again until smooth. If you don't have an immersion blender, transfer to a blender and carefully blend in batches with the lid vented to release steam.

7. Serve the soup in four bowls with a quarter of the crispy chickpeas and reserved cauliflower florets in each, along with fresh thyme and additional red pepper flakes, if desired.

LEFTOVERS: This creamy soup can easily transition to a pasta sauce. You can store the leftovers, refrigerated, for up to 5 days and combine it with cooked pasta and roasted veggies.

PER SERVING:

Calories: 390; Total Fat: 22g; Saturated Fat: 4.5g; Polyunsaturated Fat: 4g; Monounsaturated Fat: 12g; Cholesterol: 10mg; Sodium: 370mg; Carbohydrates: 36g; Fiber: 10g; Sugars: 12g; Added Sugars: 0g; Protein: 15g

SMOKED OYSTER & CLAM CHOWDER

Serves 4

PREP TIME: 10 minutes / COOK TIME: 30 minutes

GLUTEN-FREE

My husband has been a fan of smoked oysters for a long time, but I didn't appreciate them until I realized they could be used in place of bacon to create a savory, umami flavor. This recipe features this amazing flavor profile. Look for tins of smoked oysters and canned clams in the same section of the grocery store as canned tuna and salmon.

1 tablespoon canola oil

1 sweet or yellow onion, diced

3 celery stalks, cut into ¼-inch slices

2 or 3 rosemary sprigs

2 bay leaves

1 cup dry white wine

4 cups seafood stock

3 large white potatoes, diced (peel if desired)

2 (6-ounce) cans clams

1 (3-ounce) can smoked oysters

1 cup frozen or canned sweet corn kernels

8 ounces half-and-half

Salt

Freshly ground black pepper

Fresh rosemary, for garnish (optional)

1. Heat a large saucepan or Dutch oven over medium heat. Add the oil. Once the pan is glistening, add the onion, celery, rosemary, and bay leaves. Sauté for 5 to 8 minutes, or until the onion becomes translucent. Add the white wine and stir, scraping to deglaze the bottom of the pan. Cook for 3 minutes more.

2. Add the seafood stock and potatoes. Bring to a boil, then reduce heat and simmer for 15 minutes, or until the potatoes become tender. Meanwhile, drain and chop the clams and oysters.

3. After 10 minutes, carefully ladle half of the soup, liquid included, into a blender. Vent the lid to allow the steam to escape, and blend until smooth. Add the purée back to the saucepan or Dutch oven and stir to thicken.

4. Add the clams, oysters, corn, and half-and-half. Simmer for 8 minutes more. Season with salt and pepper to taste, and serve with fresh rosemary, if desired.

INGREDIENT TIP: No seafood stock? No problem. Swap for 3 cups low-sodium vegetable stock plus 1 cup clam juice or reserve the liquid from the drained clams and oysters.

PER SERVING:

Calories: 490; Total Fat: 14g; Saturated Fat: 5g; Polyunsaturated Fat: 2g; Monounsaturated Fat: 5g; Cholesterol: 50mg; Sodium: 740mg; Carbohydrates: 60g; Fiber: 8g; Sugars: 9g; Added Sugars: 0g; Protein: 21g

FISHERMAN'S STEW IN THE SLOW COOKER

Serves 4

PREP TIME: 10 minutes / COOK TIME: 4 to 6 hours

QUICK PREP

Frozen seafood is sometimes the best option for those of us living far from the coasts. The mix for this recipe can be adjusted based on availability and your budget. It's the perfect way to bring the taste from the ocean to your kitchen no matter where it is.

1 (28-ounce) can diced tomatoes

1 (6-ounce) can tomato paste, no salt added

4 cups seafood stock

3 garlic cloves, minced

½ pound new potatoes, scrubbed

1 sweet or yellow onion, diced

1 large celery stalk, cut

1 teaspoon dried thyme

1 teaspoon dried oregano

1 teaspoon dried basil

2 bay leaves

1 pound mixed frozen seafood (shrimp, scallops, mussels, crab, lobster)

1 bunch scallions, thinly sliced, for garnish

4 slices toasted French or sourdough bread

1. In the slow cooker, combine the tomatoes and their juices, tomato paste, seafood stock, garlic, potatoes, onion, celery, thyme, oregano, basil, and bay leaves. Gently stir until the tomato paste is incorporated into the mixture. Cook on high for 3 hours or on low for 4 to 5 hours, or until the potatoes are tender.

2. Meanwhile, thaw the seafood in a cold water bath, and rinse under cold running water. Remove the lid to the slow cooker and add the seafood. Cook for 30 to 60 minutes longer, or until the seafood is fully cooked.

3. Remove the bay leaves, ladle into four bowls, and garnish with the scallions. Serve with toasted French or sourdough bread.

INGREDIENT TIP: Leave in any tails or shells from the seafood mix for more robust seafood flavor during cooking. Remove and discard before serving.

PER SERVING:

Calories: 420; Total Fat: 3g; Saturated Fat: 0.5g; Polyunsaturated Fat: 1g; Monounsaturated Fat: 0.5g; Cholesterol: 85mg; Sodium: 1,410mg; Carbohydrates: 73g; Fiber: 9g; Sugars: 17g; Added Sugars: 0g; Protein: 28g

VEGETARIAN CHILI WITH BUTTERNUT SQUASH

Serves 4

PREP TIME: 10 minutes / COOK TIME: 5 to 7 hours

QUICK PREP GLUTEN-FREE VEGETARIAN

While there are endless variations of vegetarian chili, this is the version that shows up most often at my house. Make it your own by adding or substituting vegetables or spices to fit your tastes, or double the batch to have plenty of leftovers.

1 red onion, diced

1 green bell pepper, diced

1 red bell pepper, diced

2½ cups peeled and cubed butternut squash

1 (28-ounce) can crushed tomatoes

3 garlic cloves, minced

1 tablespoon chili powder

½ tablespoon ground cumin

½ teaspoon ground cayenne pepper

½ teaspoon ground cinnamon

¼ teaspoon salt

1 (15.5-ounce) can black beans, drained and rinsed

1 (15.5-ounce) can kidney beans, drained and rinsed

2 cups water

1 cup uncooked quinoa

Sour cream, for garnish (optional)

1. In the slow cooker, combine the onion, green and red bell peppers, squash, tomatoes with their juices, garlic, chili powder, cumin, cayenne pepper, cinnamon, salt, black and kidney beans, water, and quinoa, then stir gently to combine. Cook on high for 4 to 5 hours or low for 6 to 7 hours.

2. Turn the slow cooker to warm until ready to serve. Top each bowl with sour cream, if desired.

VARIATION: Add a protein boost by browning tofu crumbles and adding at the end of cooking. You can also add scallions, cilantro, fresh jalapeños, or cheese, but keep in mind that these are not included in the nutritional analysis.

PER SERVING:

Calories: 470; Total Fat: 11g; Saturated Fat: 5g; Polyunsaturated Fat: 1.5g; Monounsaturated Fat: 3g; Cholesterol: 20mg; Sodium: 870mg; Carbohydrates: 68g; Fiber: 18g; Sugars: 15g; Added Sugars: 0g; Protein: 17g

SEAFOOD GUMBO-LAYA

Serves 6

PREP TIME: 10 minutes / COOK TIME: 30 minutes

QUICK PREP GLUTEN-FREE

I admit to being aware of the differences in Cajun and Creole cuisine, but this hybrid between gumbo and jambalaya is one of our favorite one-skillet meals in my house. While I can appreciate the deep flavor that comes from a roux (a mixture of fat and flour that creates a thick, creamy texture), this recipe lets you skip that step for the convenience of getting a meal on the table more quickly.

2 tablespoons canola oil

3 celery stalks, diced

1 yellow onion, diced

1 green bell pepper, diced

3 garlic cloves, minced

2 bay leaves

1 teaspoon Creole seasoning

¼ teaspoon ground cayenne pepper

⅛ teaspoon freshly ground black pepper

½ (6-ounce) can tomato paste, no salt added

1 cup sliced frozen okra

1 (28-ounce) can crushed tomatoes

2 cups vegetable or seafood stock

1 pound peeled and deveined shrimp

½ pound bay scallops

6 cups cooked rice

Fresh parsley, for garnish (optional)

1. In a large saucepan or Dutch oven over medium-high heat, heat the oil. Add the celery, onion, bell pepper, and garlic, and cook for 2 to 3 minutes, until it becomes fragrant, then add the bay leaves, Creole seasoning, cayenne pepper, and black pepper. Stir to combine, then add the tomato paste and cook for 2 to 3 minutes more.

2. Add the okra, tomatoes with their juices, and stock. Stir to combine and simmer, covered, stirring occasionally.

3. After 20 minutes, add the shrimp and scallops. Simmer for another 3 to 4 minutes, or until the seafood is fully cooked. The shrimp and scallops should be opaque. Serve over cooked rice, and garnish with fresh parsley, if desired.

INGREDIENT TIP: Bay scallops are often smaller than sea scallops and can usually be found frozen. Be sure to fully thaw frozen scallops before adding to the pan to avoid a longer cooking time. Add seafood last to avoid an overcooked, rubbery texture.

PER SERVING:

Calories: 420; Total Fat: 6g; Saturated Fat: 0.5g; Polyunsaturated Fat: 2g; Monounsaturated Fat: 3g; Cholesterol: 80mg; Sodium: 940mg; Carbohydrates: 70g; Fiber: 5g; Sugars: 8g; Added Sugars: 0g; Protein: 19g

CREAMY CRAWFISH BISQUE

Serves 4

PREP TIME: 5 minutes / COOK TIME: 35 minutes

QUICK PREP GLUTEN-FREE

I never appreciated crawfish until the summer after we moved into our house. A neighborhood friend invited us to their annual crawfish boil, and I was hooked. He shared his tips for using the leftover crawfish tails, and that's what inspired this recipe. Look for crawfish tails in your freezer section to save the hassle of boiling and peeling.

2 tablespoons butter

1 yellow onion, diced

½ (6-ounce) can tomato paste, no salt added

½ teaspoon dried thyme

6 cups low-sodium vegetable or seafood stock

12 ounces crawfish tail meat, divided

1 (14-ounce) block silken tofu, drained

½ cup 2% cottage cheese

¼ cup half-and-half

1 tablespoon freshly squeezed lemon juice

Salt

Freshly ground black pepper

Scallions or fresh parsley, for garnish

1. In a large saucepan or Dutch oven over medium-high heat, melt the butter. Add the onion and cook for 5 minutes, or until the onions begin to soften.

2. Add the tomato paste and dried thyme, and stir to combine. Pour in the stock, scraping to deglaze the bottom of the pan. Bring to a simmer and add about half of the crawfish tails. Simmer for 15 to 20 minutes.

3. Add the silken tofu, and use an immersion blender to combine. If you don't have an immersion blender, carefully transfer to a blender and blend in batches with the lid vented to allow steam to escape.

4. Return the blended soup to the pan and cook for 5 minutes more. Stir in the cottage cheese, half-and-half, lemon juice, and the remaining crawfish tails. Cook for about 5 minutes more, until the crawfish tails curl and appear opaque, similar to cooked shrimp. Add salt and black pepper to taste. Ladle into four bowls, garnish with scallions or parsley, and serve.

VARIATION: Experiment with other types of seafood such as shrimp, crab, or lobster meat for another version of this seafood bisque.

PER SERVING:

Calories: 280; Total Fat: 12g; Saturated Fat: 6g; Polyunsaturated Fat: 2g; Monounsaturated Fat: 3g; Cholesterol: 140mg; Sodium: 1,080mg; Carbohydrates: 13g; Fiber: 1g; Sugars: 8g; Added Sugars: 0g; Protein: 30g

Roasted Root Vegetable Grain Bowls, page 87

— 6 —

VEGETARIAN MAINS

Thai Dye Bowls with Freekeh, 80

Crispy Chickpea–Stuffed Sweet Potatoes, 81

Sofritas Taco Salad Bowls, 82

Black Bean Tostadas with Off-the-Cob Street Corn, 84

Smashed Chickpea Salad Sandwiches, 85

Unstuffed Pepper Bowls, 86

Roasted Root Vegetable Grain Bowls, 87

Slow Cooker Red Curry, 88

White Bean & Kale Skillet with Quick-Fried Egg, 89

Pesto Pasta with Vegetarian Meatballs, 90

Spicy Shakshuka Breakfast-for-Dinner Skillet, 91

Grown-Up Grilled Cheese with Sun-Dried Tomatoes, 92

THAI DYE BOWLS WITH FREEKEH

Serves 4

PREP TIME: 10 minutes / COOK TIME: 20 minutes

`30 MINUTES` `VEGETARIAN`

This is a meal-prep favorite in our house. I love the spicy flavor in the sauce and the different textures of the veggies. Don't worry if you have never heard of freekeh. It is an ancient grain made from cracked wheat. Look for it in the grains or bulk section of your grocery store.

1 cup shelled edamame

Nonstick cooking spray (optional)

½ head cauliflower, chopped

3 tablespoons sesame oil, divided

2½ cups water

1 cup uncooked freekeh

1 tablespoon low-sodium soy sauce

2 tablespoons creamy peanut butter

Juice of 1 lime

1 teaspoon honey

1 teaspoon minced garlic

½ teaspoon red pepper flakes

¼ teaspoon Chinese five-spice powder

2 red bell peppers, sliced

1 cup shredded carrots

1 cup shredded red cabbage

2 scallions, thinly sliced

1. Preheat the oven to 400°F. If using frozen edamame, place in water to thaw.

2. Line a baking sheet with parchment paper or lightly spray with nonstick cooking spray. In a large bowl, toss the chopped cauliflower with 1 tablespoon of sesame oil, then spread on the baking sheet in a single layer. Roast for 20 minutes, or until fully cooked and the edges begin to brown.

3. Meanwhile, in a large saucepan, bring the water to a boil and add the freekeh. Reduce to a simmer and cook, uncovered, for 15 minutes, or until all liquid is absorbed, stirring occasionally to prevent sticking. Remove from the heat and fluff gently with a fork.

4. In a small bowl, mix the remaining 2 tablespoons of sesame oil with the soy sauce, peanut butter, lime juice, honey, garlic, red pepper flakes, and Chinese five-spice powder. Stir until smooth.

5. Build four bowls by adding a quarter of the cooked freekeh to each. Top each with the roasted cauliflower, edamame, red bell peppers, carrots, and red cabbage. Drizzle one quarter of the sauce over each bowl, top with the scallions, and serve.

LEFTOVERS: Make a large batch of the sauce and store, chilled, for up to 5 days. Use as a dressing or sauce for other mixed dishes, salads, or wraps.

PER SERVING:

Calories: 420; Total Fat: 18g; Saturated Fat: 2.5g; Polyunsaturated Fat: 6.5g; Monounsaturated Fat: 6.5g; Cholesterol: 0mg; Sodium: 240mg; Carbohydrates: 53g; Fiber: 14g; Sugars: 10g; Added Sugars: 1.5g; Protein: 16g

CRISPY CHICKPEA-STUFFED SWEET POTATOES

Serves 4

PREP TIME: 10 minutes / COOK TIME: 40 minutes

QUICK PREP GLUTEN-FREE VEGETARIAN

Stuffed sweet potatoes are an incredibly versatile vegetarian meal. Swapping a few ingredients in this recipe can completely change the flavor profile.

4 large sweet potatoes

1 (14.5-ounce) can chickpeas, drained and rinsed

½ teaspoon ground cumin

½ teaspoon red pepper flakes

½ teaspoon smoked paprika

¼ teaspoon dried sage

Salt

Freshly ground black pepper

1 tablespoon extra-virgin olive oil

½ bunch curly parsley (about 1 cup, tightly packed), large stems removed

1 cup halved cherry tomatoes

½ red onion, finely diced

2 garlic cloves, minced

Juice of 1 lemon

1 cup prepared hummus

½ cup sunflower seeds, roasted and salted

1. Preheat the oven to 400°F.

2. Wash the sweet potatoes, and pierce with a fork or knife. Place on a baking sheet and bake for 40 minutes (for medium sweet potatoes), or until tender.

3. Dry the chickpeas and add to a small bowl with the cumin, red pepper flakes, smoked paprika, and sage. Season with salt and pepper to taste. Add the olive oil and mix. Spread in a single layer on a baking sheet, and place in the oven when there are 30 minutes remaining on the potatoes. If needed, transfer the sweet potatoes to the middle rack and roast the chickpeas on the top rack.

4. Meanwhile, make a tomato-parsley salad: Coarsely chop the parsley. Add to the same small bowl along with the cherry tomatoes, onion, garlic, and lemon juice. Stir to combine, then chill until ready to serve.

5. When the sweet potatoes and chickpeas are finished baking, remove from the oven and allow to cool slightly (5 to 10 minutes). Slice each potato in half and fluff with a fork. To serve, spoon ¼ cup of hummus per potato, distributing evenly on each half. Then add the tomato-parsley salad, chickpeas, and sunflower seeds. Serve immediately.

INGREDIENT TIP: In place of hummus, you can also add a drizzle of tahini or use creamy peanut butter or almond butter instead.

PER SERVING:

Calories: 430; Total Fat: 15g; Saturated Fat: 2g; Polyunsaturated Fat: 6g; Monounsaturated Fat: 6g; Cholesterol: 0mg; Sodium: 490mg; Carbohydrates: 63g; Fiber: 15g; Sugars: 13g; Added Sugars: 0g; Protein: 15g

SOFRITAS TACO SALAD BOWLS

Serves 4

PREP TIME: 10 minutes / COOK TIME: 20 minutes

30 MINUTES GLUTEN-FREE VEGETARIAN

"Sofritas" comes from the word *sofrito*, a sauce that is a flavorful mix of peppers, onions, garlic, and tomatoes. Adjust the spice level to your taste preference in this Spanish-inspired recipe.

1 (14-ounce) block firm or extra-firm tofu

2 tablespoons extra-virgin olive oil, divided

1 tablespoon adobo sauce (from 1 can chipotles in adobo sauce)

1 Roma tomato, quartered

2 garlic cloves, peeled

1 tablespoon honey, divided

½ teaspoon salt, divided

1 teaspoon ground cumin

2 teaspoons taco seasoning

1 (15.5-ounce) can black beans, drained and rinsed

1 cup sweet corn kernels, canned or frozen

1½ cups shredded red cabbage

1½ cups shredded carrots

½ cup chopped fresh cilantro

2 scallions, thinly sliced

Juice of 1 lime

¼ teaspoon red pepper flakes

6 cups loosely packed salad greens

1. Drain the tofu, pressing to remove the liquid. Add 1 tablespoon of olive oil to a large skillet and heat the pan to medium-high heat. When the pan is heated, add the tofu and roughly crumble with a spatula to break into small pieces. Cook the tofu, uncovered, for 10 to 12 minutes: avoid too much stirring or flipping to allow for browning.

2. Meanwhile, in a blender or food processor, combine the adobo sauce, tomato, garlic, 1 teaspoon of honey, ¼ teaspoon salt, cumin, and taco seasoning. Pulse until a smooth paste begins to form. Set the sauce aside.

3. When the tofu is browned, add the sauce, black beans, and corn. Stir to combine, then allow to cook for 5 minutes more to blend the flavors. Remove from the heat.

4. To prepare the slaw, in a large mixing bowl, combine the cabbage, carrots, cilantro, and scallions. Add the remaining 1 tablespoon of olive oil, the remaining ¼ teaspoon of salt, the lime juice, red pepper flakes, and remaining 2 teaspoons of honey, and mix well to combine.

5. Allow the sofritas mixture to cool slightly after cooking. Add the salad greens to a serving bowl, spoon the sofritas mixture on top, along with the slaw, and serve.

VARIATION: Turn this recipe into tacos by serving in corn or flour tortillas instead of a bowl.

PER SERVING:

Calories: 330; Total Fat: 12g; Saturated Fat: 1.5g; Polyunsaturated Fat: 5g; Monounsaturated Fat: 4g; Cholesterol: 0mg; Sodium: 460mg; Carbohydrates: 42g; Fiber: 12g; Sugars: 14g; Added Sugars: 7g; Protein: 21g

BLACK BEAN TOSTADAS WITH OFF-THE-COB STREET CORN

Serves 4

PREP TIME: 20 minutes / COOK TIME: 20 minutes

GLUTEN-FREE VEGETARIAN

Everyone in my family is a big fan of any Mexican-inspired recipe, but we typically resort to tacos. These tostadas are a fun way to mix things up and not worry about overfilling your tortilla. We pair ours with homemade margaritas and plenty of chips to go with leftover salsa.

1 cup sweet corn kernels, canned or frozen

1 (14.5-ounce) can diced tomatoes, drained

½ tablespoon freshly squeezed lime juice

½ small red onion, finely diced

1 small jalapeño, minced

½ bunch fresh cilantro, chopped

8 small (6-inch) corn tortillas

1 teaspoon canola oil

1 (15.5-ounce) can black beans, drained and rinsed

1 teaspoon ground cumin

1 teaspoon onion powder

½ teaspoon chili powder

1 cup shredded pepper Jack cheese

1 avocado, sliced

1 lime, cut into wedges

1. To make the corn salsa, in a medium bowl, combine the corn, tomatoes, lime juice, onion, jalapeño, and cilantro. Stir, then chill in the refrigerator until ready to serve.

2. In a large nonstick skillet over medium heat, toast the tortillas until crispy. Set aside.

3. In the same skillet over medium heat, combine the canola oil, black beans, cumin, onion powder, and chili powder, and cook until heated through, about 5 minutes.

4. Assemble the tostadas by arranging the crispy tortillas on plates. Spoon the black bean mixture into the center of each, then top with the cheese. Serve immediately with the corn salsa, avocado, and wedges of lime.

SUBSTITUTION: Flour tortillas also work well in this recipe if you prefer a softer texture or wish to use this combination for tacos instead.

PER SERVING:

Calories: 340; Total Fat: 11g; Saturated Fat: 2.5g; Polyunsaturated Fat: 2g; Monounsaturated Fat: 5g; Cholesterol: 10mg; Sodium: 950mg; Carbohydrates: 50g; Fiber: 13g; Sugars: 4g; Added Sugars: 0g; Protein: 14g

SMASHED CHICKPEA SALAD SANDWICHES

Serves 4

PREP TIME: 10 minutes

QUICK PREP VEGETARIAN

Smashed chickpea salad is one of my favorite alternatives to tuna or chicken salad. I like to stack my sandwiches with leftover veggies or extra hummus or serve it on a bed of greens for a salad version.

1 (14.5-ounce) can chickpeas, drained and rinsed

1 scallion, thinly sliced

¼ cup prepared hummus

1 avocado

Pinch salt

Pinch freshly ground black pepper

8 slices whole-wheat or sprouted-grain bread

8 large lettuce leaves (Bibb or green leaf)

4 slices provolone or Gouda cheese

½ cup alfalfa sprouts

½ cucumber, thinly sliced

1. In a medium bowl, combine the chickpeas, scallions, and hummus. Using a fork or potato masher, smash the chickpeas until a thick, chunky consistency is achieved. Dice the avocado onto the chickpea mixture and fold together to combine. Season with salt and pepper.

2. To build a sandwich, arrange two lettuce leaves on the bottom slice of bread. Add one slice of cheese. Spoon a quarter of the smashed chickpea-avocado mixture onto the sandwich, and add about a quarter of the alfalfa sprouts. Stack a quarter of the sliced cucumber on top. Place the second piece of bread on top.

3. Repeat for the remaining sandwiches and serve, or store the remaining chickpea-avocado mixture in an airtight container for 2 to 3 days in the refrigerator.

VARIATION: Experiment with other sandwich toppings, such as tomatoes, cabbage, or carrots, or try using a croissant or wrap instead of sliced bread.

PER SERVING:

Calories: 420; Total Fat: 18g; Saturated Fat: 6g; Polyunsaturated Fat: 3g; Monounsaturated Fat: 7g; Cholesterol: 20mg; Sodium: 820mg; Carbohydrates: 47g; Fiber: 12g; Sugars: 7g; Added Sugars: 0g; Protein: 21g

UNSTUFFED PEPPER BOWLS

Serves 4

PREP TIME: 5 minutes / COOK TIME: 20 minutes

30 MINUTES GLUTEN-FREE VEGETARIAN

Capture all the great flavor of stuffed peppers with less work and less mess. These deconstructed bowls are great for meal prep, and the ingredients hold up well when reheated. To make an even heartier meal, try adding an egg or additional roasted veggies.

3 cups water

1½ cups uncooked quinoa

2 teaspoons canola oil

1 yellow or red onion, diced

1 red bell pepper, diced

2 garlic cloves, minced

2 teaspoons taco seasoning

½ (6-ounce) can tomato paste, no salt added

1 (15-ounce) can black beans or kidney beans

1 cup halved cherry tomatoes

4 cups loosely packed fresh spinach

⅓ cup sour cream

½ cup shredded pepper Jack cheese

Fresh cilantro, for garnish (optional)

Juice of 1 lime (optional)

1. In a medium saucepan, bring the water to a boil. Add the quinoa and cook for 15 minutes, or until all liquid is absorbed. Remove from the heat and fluff with a fork.

2. Meanwhile, in a large skillet over medium heat, heat the oil. Sauté the onion, bell pepper, and garlic for 5 to 8 minutes, until the onion becomes translucent. Add the taco seasoning and tomato paste and cook for 2 to 3 minutes more. Add the beans and cook until heated through.

3. Transfer the cooked quinoa into four bowls. Top with the vegetable-bean mixture, and arrange the cherry tomatoes and spinach on top. Then top with the sour cream and cheese. Garnish with fresh cilantro and a squeeze of lime juice, if desired, and serve.

INGREDIENT TIP: If you prefer more servings of vegetables, increase the spinach to 6 cups and cook or wilt it beforehand. You may also use frozen spinach. Thaw beforehand and squeeze to remove excess water, then reheat with the bean mixture before adding to the bowls.

PER SERVING:

Calories: 490; Total Fat: 15g; Saturated Fat: 6g; Polyunsaturated Fat: 3.5g; Monounsaturated Fat: 4.5g; Cholesterol: 25mg; Sodium: 360mg; Carbohydrates: 70g; Fiber: 14g; Sugars: 10g; Added Sugars: 0g; Protein: 21g

ROASTED ROOT VEGETABLE GRAIN BOWLS

Serves 4

PREP TIME: 10 minutes / COOK TIME: 30 minutes

GLUTEN-FREE VEGETARIAN

Root vegetables are among my favorite ingredients to use in vegetarian meals. Roasting brings out their sweetness, and they pair nicely with hearty grains such as sorghum. This recipe is another great option for meal prep and reheating for weekday lunches.

1 (8-ounce) package white or baby bella mushrooms, quartered

2 turnips, peeled and cut into half-moons

2 large carrots, peeled and sliced

1 golden beet, cut into ½-inch cubes

1 red beet, cut into ½-inch cubes

1 cup uncooked pearled sorghum

Pinch salt

Pinch freshly ground black pepper

1 tablespoon extra-virgin olive oil

4 teaspoons balsamic vinegar

½ cup crumbled goat cheese

Fresh rosemary, stripped from stems, for garnish (optional)

1. Preheat the oven to 400°F.

2. On a large baking sheet, arrange the mushrooms, turnips, carrots, and golden and red beets in a single layer. Roast for 25 to 30 minutes, or until fully cooked. Remove the mushrooms early if needed to prevent burning.

3. Meanwhile, in a medium saucepan, cook the sorghum in water according to the package instructions, simmering for 15 to 20 minutes, or until all liquid is absorbed. Remove from the heat, fluff with a fork, and season with salt and pepper.

4. To serve, distribute the roasted vegetables and mushrooms evenly among four plates. Add the cooked sorghum on top, and drizzle with the olive oil and balsamic vinegar. Top with the goat cheese and rosemary, if desired, and serve.

INGREDIENT TIP: Look for sorghum in the health section or bulk bins in your grocery store. Online ordering is also an option, or you can substitute another grain such as farro, freekeh, or Israeli couscous.

PER SERVING:

Calories: 490; Total Fat: 13g; Saturated Fat: 5g; Polyunsaturated Fat: 2g; Monounsaturated Fat: 5g; Cholesterol: 15mg; Sodium: 380mg; Carbohydrates: 84g; Fiber: 10g; Sugars: 11g; Added Sugars: 0g; Protein: 19g

SLOW COOKER RED CURRY

Serves 6

PREP TIME: 15 minutes / COOK TIME: 3 hours 10 minutes

GLUTEN-FREE **VEGETARIAN**

This slow cooker meal can be prepped in no time flat. Prepare the rice ahead of time as part of your meal-prep routine, or use frozen or minute rice to reduce prep time even more.

1 sweet potato, washed and cut into ½-inch cubes

½ pound green beans, trimmed and cut into 1-inch pieces

1 red bell pepper, sliced

2 large carrots, peeled and cut into ¼- to ½-inch coins

1 tablespoon canola oil

1 yellow onion, sliced

3 tablespoons red curry paste

1 garlic clove, minced

1 teaspoon ground ginger

1 (13-ounce) can coconut milk

1 tablespoon low-sodium soy sauce

1 tablespoon tightly packed brown sugar

1 (14-ounce) block firm or extra-firm tofu, drained and cut into ½-inch cubes

6 cups cooked brown rice

1 small bunch fresh basil, chopped

Juice of 1 lime (optional)

1. In the slow cooker, combine the sweet potato, green beans, bell pepper, and carrots.

2. In a medium skillet over medium heat, heat the oil. Add the onion and cook for 5 to 8 minutes, or until the onion becomes translucent. Add the curry paste, garlic, and ginger and cook for 1 minute more. Stir in the coconut milk, soy sauce, and brown sugar, and stir to combine. Bring to a simmer, then quickly remove from the heat and pour over the vegetables in the slow cooker.

3. Cook on low for 3 hours. At the end of cooking, add the tofu to the curry mixture. Put 1 cup of the cooked rice in each serving bowl, then spoon the curry mixture on top. Garnish with the chopped basil and a squeeze of lime juice, if desired, and serve.

LEFTOVERS: Store leftovers in the fridge for up to 5 days or portion into single-serving containers and freeze for up to 3 months. Defrost overnight in the fridge, then reheat by microwaving in 30-second increments.

PER SERVING:

Calories: 530; Total Fat: 22g; Saturated Fat: 13g; Polyunsaturated Fat: 4g; Monounsaturated Fat: 4g; Cholesterol: 0mg; Sodium: 330mg; Carbohydrates: 70g; Fiber: 10g; Sugars: 12g; Added Sugars: 2g; Protein: 17g

WHITE BEAN & KALE SKILLET WITH QUICK-FRIED EGG

Serves 4

PREP TIME: 5 minutes / COOK TIME: 25 minutes

30 MINUTES VEGETARIAN

I love a one-skillet meal because it has a short cleanup time. This one also has a quick prep time and can double as a breakfast meal—it's extremely versatile!

2 tablespoons extra-virgin olive oil, divided

1 tablespoon low-sodium soy sauce

1 (8-ounce) package tempeh, cut into cubes or coarsely crumbled

1 large bunch kale, shredded

1 garlic clove, minced

Pinch salt

Pinch freshly ground black pepper

¼ teaspoon red pepper flakes

1 (15.5-ounce) can white beans (great northern or cannellini), drained and rinsed

4 large eggs

1. In a large skillet over medium-high heat, heat 1 tablespoon of olive oil with the soy sauce. Add the tempeh, and stir until coated. Allow to cook until the tempeh begins to crisp, 5 to 8 minutes, stirring occasionally. Transfer the tempeh to a plate and cover to keep warm.

2. In the same skillet over medium-high heat, heat the remaining 1 tablespoon of olive oil. Add the kale, garlic, salt, pepper, and red pepper flakes. Cook, covered, for 5 to 6 minutes, or until the kale softens and becomes a dark, vibrant green color. Stir in the beans and heat through, cooking uncovered for about 3 minutes more.

3. Divide the kale mixture evenly among four bowls, and top with the cooked tempeh. In the same skillet, prepare the quick-fried eggs (cooked over-easy to over-medium). Top each bowl with one egg and serve immediately.

VARIATION: Replace the kale with Swiss chard or spinach when available. For a heartier meal, add a second egg to each serving for a total of 8 eggs.

PER SERVING:

Calories: 410; Total Fat: 19g; Saturated Fat: 4g; Polyunsaturated Fat: 4.5g; Monounsaturated Fat: 9g; Cholesterol: 185mg; Sodium: 370mg; Carbohydrates: 36g; Fiber: 13g; Sugars: 5g; Added Sugars: 0g; Protein: 29g

PESTO PASTA WITH VEGETARIAN MEATBALLS

Serves 6

PREP TIME: 20 minutes / COOK TIME: 25 minutes

VEGETARIAN

I take advantage during warm summer months when fresh basil is abundant. I'll prep batches to store in the freezer so I can enjoy pesto with recipes all year long. This version features vegetarian meatballs but can also pair well with shrimp or salmon.

1 (12-ounce) box thin spaghetti or linguine pasta

2 tablespoons extra-virgin olive oil, divided

2 (8-ounce) packages white or baby bella mushrooms

1¼ cups prepared pesto

1 cup frozen green peas, thawed

4 cups loosely packed fresh spinach

Nonstick cooking spray (optional)

1 cup uncooked quick oats

½ cup bread crumbs

½ cup grated Parmesan cheese

2 large eggs

1½ teaspoons Italian seasoning

½ teaspoon red pepper flakes

1. Cook the pasta according to package instructions or al dente (firm to the bite). While the pasta cooks, in a large skillet over medium-low heat, heat 1 tablespoon of olive oil. Add the mushrooms and cook until most liquid is released, about 10 minutes. Continue cooking until the mushrooms are browned, then remove and pat dry.

2. When the pasta is ready, turn off the heat, drain, then stir in the pesto sauce, green peas, and spinach. The heat from the cooked pasta will wilt the spinach, so continue stirring until well incorporated. Keep warm while you prepare the meatballs.

3. Preheat the oven to 400°F. Line a baking sheet with parchment paper or spray with nonstick cooking spray.

4. In a food processor, combine the mushrooms, oats, bread crumbs, Parmesan cheese, eggs, Italian seasoning, the remaining 1 tablespoon of olive oil, and red pepper flakes. Pulse until a dough-like texture forms. Then, form into balls and place on the prepared baking sheet.

5. Bake for 15 minutes, or until the outsides begin to brown. Remove from the oven and serve with the pasta.

LEFTOVERS: Make a double batch of the meatballs to store for later. Allow to cool completely, then layer in a zip-top bag with parchment paper between layers and freeze for up to 3 months.

PER SERVING:

Calories: 670; Total Fat: 34g; Saturated Fat: 7g; Polyunsaturated Fat: 3.5g; Monounsaturated Fat: 18g; Cholesterol: 70mg; Sodium: 730mg; Carbohydrates: 70g; Fiber: 8g; Sugars: 7g; Added Sugars: 0g; Protein: 22g

SPICY SHAKSHUKA BREAKFAST-FOR-DINNER SKILLET

Serves 4

PREP TIME: 5 minutes / COOK TIME: 30 minutes

VEGETARIAN GLUTEN-FREE

Shakshuka is a delicious dish of eggs poached in a tomato-based sauce. It has Middle Eastern and West African influences, so you can bring global flavor to your table using familiar ingredients.

1 tablespoon extra-virgin olive oil

1 yellow onion, thinly sliced

1 red bell pepper, thinly sliced

2 garlic cloves, minced

1 teaspoon ground cumin

1 teaspoon smoked paprika

¼ teaspoon ground cayenne pepper

1 cup halved cherry tomatoes

2 cups prepared marinara sauce

2 cups tightly packed fresh baby spinach

Salt

Freshly ground black pepper

4 large eggs

½ cup feta or goat cheese crumbles

¼ cup fresh chopped parsley, for garnish

1. Preheat the oven to 375°F.

2. In a large cast iron or oven-safe skillet over medium heat, heat the olive oil. Add the onion and bell pepper and sauté for 10 to 15 minutes, or until the onion begins to caramelize. Add the garlic and cook until fragrant, about 1 minute. Add the cumin, smoked paprika, and cayenne pepper, and stir to combine. Add the cherry tomatoes and marinara sauce and mix well.

3. Add the spinach and allow it to wilt, about 3 to 5 minutes. Season with salt and black pepper to taste.

4. Using a spoon, make 4 small indentations in the sauce mixture. Carefully crack one egg at a time into a small bowl or cup, then slide the cracked egg into an indentation. Repeat with the remaining eggs. Do not stir or cover the eggs, and avoid breaking the yolks.

5. Sprinkle the cheese over the eggs and bake for 7 to 10 minutes, or until the eggs are set but still wobbly. Remove the skillet from the oven and top with the parsley. Serve immediately.

SERVING SUGGESTION: Serve one egg with sauce per serving, pairing it with your favorite naan or pita bread. For a heartier meal, add 4 more eggs to the recipe, for a total of 8 eggs.

PER SERVING:

Calories: 270; Total Fat: 15g; Saturated Fat: 5g; Polyunsaturated Fat: 2g; Monounsaturated Fat: 6g; Cholesterol: 205mg; Sodium: 310mg; Carbohydrates: 24g; Fiber: 5g; Sugars: 15g; Added Sugars: 0g; Protein: 13g

GROWN-UP GRILLED CHEESE WITH SUN-DRIED TOMATOES

Serves 4

PREP TIME: 5 minutes / COOK TIME: 1 hour 15 minutes

VEGETARIAN

Caramelized onions are one of my all-time favorite ingredients. They do take time to make, but the effort is worth it for the savory-sweet flavor they add to every dish you use them in. If you prefer to skip that lengthy step, look for an onion jam or spread to use instead.

1 tablespoon extra-virgin olive oil

1 large onion, sliced (whatever variety you prefer)

8 slices sandwich bread or sourdough

8 slices Havarti cheese

½ cup sun-dried tomatoes, sliced or chopped

1 cup loosely packed fresh spinach

1. In a medium nonstick skillet over medium heat, heat the olive oil. Add the onion and cook for 40 to 60 minutes. The onion will turn a deep golden brown color and reduce in volume the longer it cooks. When finished, remove from the heat and allow to cool.

2. Build your sandwich by layering the onion on the top and bottom slice of bread. Add one slice of cheese to each half. Place the sun-dried tomatoes on one side and the spinach on the other, then carefully close the sandwich.

3. In the skillet over medium heat, cook for 2 to 4 minutes on each side, or until the bread is toasted to your desired level and the cheese is melted. Cut in half and serve immediately.

SUBSTITUTION: Havarti cheese is known as a great cheese for melting, but if you don't have it available you can also use provolone, Gouda, or sliced mozzarella cheese.

PER SERVING:

Calories: 520; Total Fat: 20g; Saturated Fat: 11g; Polyunsaturated Fat: 2g; Monounsaturated Fat: 3g; Cholesterol: 40mg; Sodium: 580mg; Carbohydrates: 61g; Fiber: 4g; Sugars: 7g; Added Sugars: 0g; Protein: 25g

Pan-Seared Trout with Edamame Succotash, page 114

SEAFOOD MAINS

LEMON-HERB BAKED SHRIMP WITH PASTA

Serves 4

PREP TIME: 10 minutes / COOK TIME: 20 minutes
30 MINUTES

It's no secret; I'm a huge pasta lover. It's often our go-to quick dinner because it's easy and cheap, and it makes great leftovers for weekday lunches. Try adding other vegetables or seasonings to your version of this simple, but flavorful, recipe.

½ cup extra-virgin olive oil

4 or 5 rosemary sprigs

2 teaspoons fresh oregano

10 to 12 garlic cloves, peeled

¼ teaspoon red pepper flakes

¼ teaspoon salt

¼ teaspoon freshly ground black pepper

1 lemon, halved then sliced, divided

1 small head broccoli

1 pound large shrimp, peeled and deveined

12 ounces uncooked thin spaghetti or linguine

1. Preheat the oven to 400°F. Pour the olive oil into a large baking dish.

2. In the baking dish, combine the rosemary, oregano, garlic, red pepper flakes, salt, black pepper, and half of the sliced lemons. Bake for 10 minutes, or until fragrant. Meanwhile, wash and chop the broccoli into bite-size florets.

3. Remove the baking dish from the oven. Layer the broccoli and shrimp over the top of the herb mix. Gently toss until everything is evenly coated. Top with the remaining lemon slices and bake for an additional 10 minutes, or until the shrimp are pink and opaque.

4. Meanwhile, bring a large pot of water to a boil and cook the pasta according to the package directions for al dente (firm to the bite). Add the cooked pasta to the baking dish after removing it from the oven. Gently toss to fully combine. Serve immediately.

SUBSTITUTION: Baking the herbs with the olive oil infuses more flavor into the final dish, but if you prefer to skip this step, you can just use a bottle of infused oil. These are usually found in the health food sections of most grocery stores or local culinary shops.

PER SERVING:

Calories: 460; Total Fat: 20g; Saturated Fat: 3g; Polyunsaturated Fat: 2.5g; Monounsaturated Fat: 13.5g; Cholesterol: 96mg; Sodium: 520mg; Carbohydrates: 51g; Fiber: 4g; Sugars: 3g; Added Sugars: 0g; Protein: 20g

MEDITERRANEAN SALMON WRAPS

Serves 4

PREP TIME: 10 minutes

QUICK PREP

This simple recipe is perfect for pack-and-go lunches or quick dinners on busy week-nights. You can use the same salmon mix to build sandwiches, lettuce wraps, and salads when you aren't in the mood for a wrap. And the leftovers taste even better once the flavors have a chance to mingle.

2 (6-ounce) cans salmon, drained

¼ cup chopped fresh parsley

¼ cup pitted Kalamata olives, chopped

¼ cup diced red onion

1 tablespoon extra-virgin olive oil

½ teaspoon lemon zest

Juice of 1 lemon

⅛ teaspoon coarse sea salt

4 small (6-inch) whole-wheat tortillas

2 cups chopped romaine

½ cup diced red bell pepper

1 Roma tomato, thinly sliced

½ cup feta cheese crumbles

1. In a large bowl, combine the salmon, parsley, olives, onion, olive oil, lemon zest, and lemon juice. Season with salt, and stir to combine.

2. Layer ½ cup chopped romaine in the center of each tortilla. Top with a quarter each of the salmon mixture and bell peppers and two slices of tomato. Sprinkle with the feta cheese.

3. Fold in each tortilla about 1 inch from the end of the filling on each side. Tightly roll, being careful not to break the wrap. Secure the edge of the wrap underneath, then cut in half. Serve immediately.

LEFTOVERS: If prepping for lunches, make salmon mix and prepare the veggies but don't roll the wraps until you're ready to serve. This will help you avoid an overly soggy wrap that tears or breaks open.

PER SERVING:

Calories: 210; Total Fat: 16g; Saturated Fat: 3.5g; Polyunsaturated Fat: 3.5g; Monounsaturated Fat: 4.5g; Cholesterol: 70mg; Sodium: 990mg; Carbohydrates: 39g; Fiber: 6g; Sugars: 4g; Added Sugars: 0g; Protein: 26g

GRILLED SWORDFISH WITH CHIMICHURRI & ROASTED VEGETABLES

Serves 4

PREP TIME: 10 minutes / **COOK TIME:** 20 minutes

30 MINUTES GLUTEN-FREE

Although swordfish is a high-mercury fish, consuming it on occasion does not pose a health threat. It is among the meatiest of all species of fish, so if you prefer a firmer texture and less fishy flavor, you'll enjoy this hearty recipe.

½ cup tightly packed chopped fresh parsley

¼ cup coarsely chopped fresh oregano

1 cup diced red onion, divided

4 garlic cloves, peeled

¼ cup red wine vinegar

½ cup extra-virgin olive oil plus 1½ tablespoons, divided, and more for brushing

1 tablespoon red pepper flakes

Salt

Freshly ground black pepper

1 zucchini, halved lengthwise and sliced

1 small head cauliflower, cut into florets

1 large carrot, trimmed and peeled, then sliced

4 (6-ounce) swordfish steaks

1. For the chimichurri sauce (see page 98), add the herbs to a food processor along with ½ cup of red onion, the garlic, red wine vinegar, ½ cup of olive oil, red pepper flakes, salt, and black pepper. Pulse several times, until combined, leaving some chunks in the mixture. Transfer to a ramekin or serving bowl to allow the flavors to combine.

2. Preheat the oven to 400°F.

3. In a large bowl, toss the zucchini, cauliflower, carrot, the remaining ½ cup of red onion, and 1½ tablespoons of olive oil. Season with salt and black pepper. Arrange in a single layer on a large baking sheet, and roast for 15 to 20 minutes, to your preferred doneness.

4. Meanwhile, heat the grill or a stove-top grill pan to medium-high heat. Brush the swordfish steaks with olive oil, and season with salt and pepper. Grill for 5 to 6 minutes on each side, depending on thickness.

5. Put one swordfish steak on each plate with a quarter of the vegetables. Top with the chimichurri sauce and serve immediately.

SERVING SUGGESTION: Roasting on high heat brings out the natural sweetness in vegetables. In a recipe like this, you may prefer to avoid strong seasonings, but you can always prepare additional chimichurri sauce to serve on top of the vegetables or use for dipping.

PER SERVING:

Calories: 600; Total Fat: 43g; Saturated Fat: 7g; Polyunsaturated Fat: 5.5g; Monounsaturated Fat: 27g; Cholesterol: 110mg; Sodium: 260mg; Carbohydrates: 19g; Fiber: 7g; Sugars: 7g; Added Sugars: 0g; Protein: 38g

SHRIMP FRIED RICE-STYLE FREEKEH

Serves 4

PREP TIME: 5 minutes / COOK TIME: 25 minutes

30 MINUTES

Growing up in a small town, Chinese carryout wasn't always an available option. As a result, our family made do with a homemade version of fried rice using simple ingredients like leftover veggies or precooked rice. My current favorite version uses freekeh, an ancient grain made from cracked wheat. The texture is hearty, but fluffy enough to be reminiscent of traditional fried rice.

1½ cups uncooked cracked freekeh

3 large eggs, lightly beaten

1½ tablespoons sesame oil

1½ cups frozen peas and carrots, thawed

⅓ pound snow peas, trimmed and chopped into bite-size pieces

2 garlic cloves, minced

1½ tablespoons low-sodium soy sauce

1 teaspoon ground ginger

1 tablespoon Sriracha hot sauce

1 pound shrimp, peeled and deveined

2 scallions, thinly sliced

1. Cook the freekeh according to package instructions. Remove from the heat and fluff with a fork.

2. Meanwhile, heat a large skillet over medium-high heat. Scramble the eggs, breaking into small chunks with your spatula. Once cooked, transfer to a plate and hold warm until needed.

3. In the same skillet, heat the sesame oil and stir-fry the peas and carrots and snow peas until the carrots are golden, about 5 minutes. Add the cooked freekeh and garlic, and season with soy sauce, ginger, and Sriracha. Increase the heat to high, then add the shrimp. Cook for 3 to 4 minutes, or until the shrimp become pink and firm. Remove from the heat.

4. Stir in the eggs and scallions. Adjust the flavor as needed and serve immediately.

INGREDIENT TIP: When shopping for freekeh, look for it near the other grains or bulk bins in your grocery store. Be sure to purchase the cracked version to keep cooking time short.

PER SERVING:

Calories: 480; Total Fat: 13g; Saturated Fat: 2.5g; Polyunsaturated Fat: 4g; Monounsaturated Fat: 4.5g; Cholesterol: 280mg; Sodium: 960mg; Carbohydrates: 58g; Fiber: 13g; Sugars: 4g; Added Sugars: 0g; Protein: 32g

BLACKENED FISH TACOS WITH CRUNCHY CORN SALSA

Serves 4

PREP TIME: 10 minutes / COOK TIME: 10 minutes

30 MINUTES

Fish tacos are one of the things I love to see on restaurant menus. I've had a lot of great fish tacos but keep coming back to the blackened version when I make them at home—I don't want to mess with the hassle of frying. And this recipe lets me use less expensive frozen fish without sacrificing great flavor.

FOR THE FISH AND TACOS

1 pound whitefish fillets, thawed

1½ tablespoons extra-virgin olive oil

2 tablespoons Jamaican jerk seasoning

¼ teaspoon freshly ground black pepper

Pinch salt

8 small (6-inch) flour tortillas

FOR THE CORN SALSA

1 cup sweet corn kernels

1 cup canned black beans, drained and rinsed

1 cup jicama, peeled and diced or cut into matchsticks

½ red onion, finely diced

½ red bell pepper, diced

½ cup chopped fresh cilantro

Juice of 1 lime

FOR THE SAUCE

¼ cup plain, low-fat Greek yogurt

¼ cup chopped fresh cilantro

½ jalapeño pepper, minced

½ teaspoon ground cumin

½ teaspoon garlic powder

TO MAKE THE FISH

1. Preheat the oven to broil. Line a baking sheet with aluminum foil.

2. Place the whitefish fillets on the baking sheet and brush with the olive oil. Generously coat with jerk seasoning and black pepper. Season with salt. Broil for 6 to 8 minutes, depending on the thickness. Once fully cooked and flaky, remove from oven and allow to cool slightly.

TO MAKE THE CORN SALSA

In a large bowl, mix the sweet corn, black beans, jicama, onion, bell pepper, cilantro, and lime juice. Set aside.

TO MAKE THE SAUCE

In another large bowl, combine the Greek yogurt, cilantro, jalapeño pepper, cumin, and garlic powder. Set aside.

continued

TO PREPARE THE TACOS

When ready to serve, flake the fish apart with a fork and place inside the toasted flour tortillas. Top with the corn salsa and sauce. Serve immediately.

VARIATION: This recipe can also be made with shrimp or salmon. Adjust the cook time as needed.

PER SERVING:

Calories: 490; Total Fat: 15g; Saturated Fat: 3g; Polyunsaturated Fat: 5g; Monounsaturated Fat: 7.5g; Cholesterol: 70mg; Sodium: 700mg; Carbohydrates: 54g; Fiber: 10g; Sugars: 5g; Added Sugars: 0g; Protein: 34g

SALMON BURGERS WITH CRUNCHY CABBAGE SLAW

Serves 4

PREP TIME: 10 minutes / COOK TIME: 10 minutes

30 MINUTES

Canned salmon is a pantry staple at our house for this specific recipe. Salmon burgers were something we enjoyed on a regular basis growing up, and that hasn't changed now that I'm the one doing the cooking. They're a quick weeknight dinner and can be prepared in batches for weekday lunches.

FOR THE CABBAGE SLAW

1½ cups shredded red cabbage

1½ cups shredded carrots

½ cup chopped fresh cilantro

2 scallions, thinly sliced

Juice of 1 lime

1½ tablespoons extra-virgin olive oil

¼ teaspoon salt

¼ teaspoon red pepper flakes

2 teaspoons honey

FOR THE SALMON BURGERS

2 large eggs

1 (12-ounce) can salmon, drained

½ cup whole-wheat bread crumbs

½ teaspoon garlic powder

½ teaspoon Old Bay seasoning

¼ teaspoon salt

¼ cup canola oil, for frying

TO MAKE THE CABBAGE SLAW

In a large bowl, combine the cabbage, carrots, cilantro, and scallions. Add the lime juice, olive oil, salt, red pepper flakes, and honey, and mix well to combine. Cover and refrigerate until ready to serve.

TO MAKE THE SALMON BURGERS

1. In another large bowl, lightly beat the eggs. Add the salmon, bread crumbs, garlic powder, Old Bay seasoning, and salt. Stir to combine, then shape into 4 equal-size patties.

2. In a large skillet over medium-high heat, heat the canola oil. Once the oil is heated, place the patties into the skillet and cook for 3 to 4 minutes on each side. If the pan is overcrowded, panfry in two batches.

3. Serve the burgers with the cabbage slaw, and store leftovers for up to 3 days.

VARIATION: Canned salmon is often mild in flavor, especially when compared with fresh or frozen varieties. Pair other seasoning mixes such as lemon pepper, curry powder, or jerk seasoning instead of Old Bay for a different take on this simple recipe.

PER SERVING:

Calories: 340; Total Fat: 18g; Saturated Fat: 2.5g; Polyunsaturated Fat: 5g; Monounsaturated Fat: 8.5g; Cholesterol: 165mg; Sodium: 830mg; Carbohydrates: 20g; Fiber: 3g; Sugars: 17g; Added Sugars: 3g; Protein: 25g

LOBSTER ROLL IN A BOWL

Serves 4

PREP TIME: 10 minutes / COOK TIME: 10 minutes

30 MINUTES

On our first trip to the East Coast, my husband and I couldn't get enough of lobster rolls. When we returned to the Midwest, fresh lobster was obviously a little harder to source. We can sometimes find it at a good price through local markets, but frozen options are the most reliable. This version lets us enjoy more of the lobster texture and flavor while still keeping the elements of a traditional lobster roll.

4 brioche buns, cut into 1-inch cubes

2 tablespoons melted butter

1 teaspoon garlic powder

12 ounces frozen lobster meat, thawed and drained

1 celery stalk, diced

¼ cup mayonnaise

1 teaspoon lemon zest

Juice of ½ lemon

1 scallion, thinly sliced

Pinch salt

Pinch freshly ground black pepper

8 cups romaine lettuce, shredded or chopped

1. Preheat the oven to 300°F.

2. Brush the cubed brioche buns with the melted butter, and season with garlic powder. Arrange on a baking sheet in a single layer and toast, flipping if needed, until crisp, about 10 minutes. Remove from the oven and set aside.

3. Meanwhile, in a large bowl, mix the lobster, celery, mayonnaise, lemon zest, lemon juice, and scallion together. Season with salt and pepper.

4. Divide the lettuce among four bowls, and top each with the lobster mixture. Top with the toasted croutons and serve immediately.

SUBSTITUTION: Lobster can, admittedly, be a splurge for most of us. This recipe also works well with shrimp, crabmeat, or leftover fish from previous recipes. Just be careful not to mix too vigorously, or the pieces may break into tiny chunks.

PER SERVING:

Calories: 470; Total Fat: 22g; Saturated Fat: 7g; Polyunsaturated Fat: 7.5g; Monounsaturated Fat: 6g; Cholesterol: 215mg; Sodium: 930mg; Carbohydrates: 43g; Fiber: 3g; Sugars: 2g; Added Sugars: 0g; Protein: 26g

CLASSIC CRAB CAKES WITH OLD BAY OVEN FRIES & AIOLI

Serves 4

PREP TIME: 15 minutes, plus 30 to 60 minutes to chill / COOK TIME: 35 minutes

This might be the most splurge-worthy recipe in the book. It's not often that I spring for the premium price of lump crabmeat, but you can also find crabmeat in cans or pouches for a lower cost. If you have a slow evening and the time to spare, I promise you this recipe is worth it. The aioli has a bit of a kick but can be made to fit your taste preferences and pairs well with just about any seafood recipe. Use it as a dipping sauce or for a condiment or spread for sandwiches and wraps. Be aware that crab is one of the few foods that is naturally high in sodium. Although the total sodium content for this recipe is higher than what is typically recommended, it can still be enjoyed occasionally. If you have been advised to follow a low-sodium diet, please refer to the substitution tip.

FOR THE CRAB CAKES

2 celery stalks, finely chopped

2 scallions, thinly sliced

2 garlic cloves, minced

2 teaspoons Dijon mustard

1 teaspoon freshly squeezed lemon juice

1 teaspoon hot sauce

2 large eggs

2 tablespoons mayonnaise

1 pound lump crabmeat

1 cup panko bread crumbs, plus ½ cup for breading

¼ cup canola oil

FOR THE OLD BAY OVEN FRIES

3 large russet potatoes, cut into ¼-inch to ½-inch matchsticks

2 tablespoons canola oil

1 teaspoon Old Bay seasoning

FOR THE AIOLI

2 large egg yolks

¼ cup freshly squeezed lemon juice

½ teaspoon garlic powder

⅛ teaspoon sugar

1 teaspoon hot sauce

¾ cup extra-virgin olive oil

continued

TO MAKE THE CRAB CAKES

1. In a large bowl, combine the celery, scallions, garlic, Dijon mustard, lemon juice, hot sauce, eggs, and mayonnaise. Stir to combine, then add the crabmeat and 1 cup of panko bread crumbs, folding only until combined to avoid breaking apart the pieces of crabmeat and overmixing. Shape into 8½-inch-thick patties, and place on a baking sheet. Loosely cover and chill in the refrigerator for 30 to 60 minutes.

2. After chilling, remove from refrigerator. In a large nonstick or cast iron skillet, heat the canola oil. Use the remaining ½ cup of panko bread crumbs to coat the crab cakes and form a thin breading. Once the oil is hot, place the crab cakes in the skillet and cook for 3 to 5 minutes on each side. Take care when flipping the crab cakes to avoid breaking them apart in the pan.

TO MAKE THE OLD BAY OVEN FRIES

Preheat the oven to 425°F. Toss the russet potatoes with the canola oil and Old Bay seasoning, then arrange in a single layer on a baking sheet. Bake for 20 minutes, flipping the potatoes halfway through. Flip a second time, and turn the oven setting to broil. Bake for 3 to 5 minutes more, or until the fries begin to crisp.

TO MAKE THE AIOLI AND SERVE

1. In a medium bowl, mix the egg yolks, lemon juice, garlic powder, sugar, and hot sauce. Then, while whisking constantly, drizzle the olive oil into the mixture and continue whisking until smooth. The aioli sauce will stay fresh for up to 3 days in the refrigerator. (Note: Consuming raw or undercooked meats, poultry, seafood, shellfish, or eggs may increase your risk of foodborne illness.)

2. Serve the crab cakes with the Old Bay oven fries and aioli.

SUBSTITUTION: Classic Old Bay seasoning is very high in sodium. If you prefer to opt for a less salty seasoning, look for salt-free seafood blends, usually available in the spice or baking aisle of most grocery stores. Substituting 1 teaspoon of a salt-free blend will reduce the overall amount of sodium by 160mg.

PER SERVING:

Calories: 780; Total Fat: 42g; Saturated Fat: 5.5g; Polyunsaturated Fat: 9g; Monounsaturated Fat: 25.5g; Cholesterol: 200mg; Sodium: 1,640mg; Carbohydrates: 65g; Fiber: 8g; Sugars: 6g; Added Sugars: 0.5g; Protein: 34g

PISTACHIO-CRUSTED SHRIMP & GRITS

Serves 4

PREP TIME: 10 minutes / COOK TIME: 10 minutes

30 MINUTES

One of my all-time favorite comfort food dishes is shrimp and grits. I love trying different versions of this Southern staple when I'm traveling. I find it fun trying to recreate my favorites in my kitchen. This version uses a simple breading and baked shrimp so you can keep your hands free to prepare the cheesy grits.

2 large eggs, lightly beaten

½ cup bread crumbs

½ cup finely chopped pistachios

½ teaspoon garlic powder

Pinch salt

Pinch freshly ground black pepper

1 pound raw shrimp, peeled and deveined, tails on

2 cups low-sodium vegetable stock

2 cups water

1 cup stone-ground grits

1½ cups shredded Cheddar cheese

2 tablespoons butter

Hot sauce, for garnish (optional)

1. Preheat the oven to 425°F. Line a baking sheet with parchment paper or aluminum foil.

2. In a small bowl, whisk the eggs for the egg wash. In a medium bowl, combine the bread crumbs, pistachios, garlic powder, salt, and pepper, and place the bowls side by side. Pat the shrimp dry. Holding them by the tails, dip into the egg wash, then coat with the pistachio mixture. Place on the baking sheet and repeat with the remaining shrimp. Bake for 8 minutes, or until the shrimp are firm and opaque.

3. Meanwhile, in a medium saucepan, bring the vegetable stock and water to a boil. Once boiling, add the grits and reduce the heat to a simmer. Stirring often, allow the grits to thicken, about 5 minutes. Remove from heat, then stir in the cheese and butter. Cover and set aside until ready to serve.

4. To serve, spoon the grits into four bowls and arrange the shrimp on top. Garnish with hot sauce, if desired.

VARIATION: Grits aren't the most common of pantry items, so use another grain like rice, orzo, or an ancient grain if you prefer. Although it will no longer be shrimp and grits in name, you will avoid purchasing a specialty ingredient.

PER SERVING:

Calories: 600; Total Fat: 30g; Saturated Fat: 14g; Polyunsaturated Fat: 3.5g; Monounsaturated Fat: 10g; Cholesterol: 250mg; Sodium: 1,280mg; Carbohydrates: 46g; Fiber: 5g; Sugars: 4g; Added Sugars: 0g; Protein: 36g

HEARTLAND HARVEST TUNA MELTS

Serves 4

PREP TIME: 10 minutes / COOK TIME: 5 minutes

30 MINUTES

This open-faced sandwich is an updated version of the classic tuna melt. As much as I love a juicy, ripe tomato for summer versions, I turn to sun-dried tomatoes the rest of the year. Look for them next to other prepared salad toppings. If using an oil-packed version, be sure to drain them before chopping.

4 thick slices of rye or whole-wheat bread

2 (5-ounce) cans tuna, drained

¼ cup 2% cottage cheese

¼ to ⅓ cup chopped sun-dried tomatoes

1 Gala or Fuji apple, peeled and thinly sliced

4 slices sharp Cheddar cheese

1. Preheat the oven broiler, and line a baking sheet with aluminum foil.

2. Lightly toast the bread, then place on the baking sheet.

3. In a large bowl, mix the tuna, cottage cheese, and sun-dried tomatoes. Build the sandwiches by layering the apples on the bottom and topping with the tuna mixture. Place the cheese on top, then broil for 5 minutes, or until the cheese is fully melted. Serve hot.

SERVING SUGGESTION: Pair with other seasonal fruit or a side salad to complete your meal. You may also top the sandwich with a second slice of toasted bread if desired, although it is not included in the nutritional analysis.

PER SERVING:

Calories: 360; Total Fat: 13g; Saturated Fat: 7g; Polyunsaturated Fat: 1.5g; Monounsaturated Fat: 4g; Cholesterol: 65mg; Sodium: 750mg; Carbohydrates: 25g; Fiber: 3g; Sugars: 8g; Added Sugars: 0g; Protein: 32g

SHRIMP & SCALLOP SKEWERS WITH CHIMICHURRI SAUCE

Serves 4

PREP TIME: 10 minutes / **COOK TIME:** 10 minutes

`30 MINUTES` `GLUTEN-FREE`

Chimichurri sauce is a traditional South American condiment often paired with steak. Key ingredients for chimichurri are garlic, oregano, and parsley. I prefer to use mine for seafood and vegetables, but it's versatile enough to pair with nearly anything.

FOR THE CHIMICHURRI SAUCE

½ cup fresh parsley, washed and chopped

¼ cup fresh oregano, washed and chopped

½ cup red onion, diced

4 garlic cloves, peeled

¼ cup red wine vinegar

½ cup extra-virgin olive oil

1 tablespoon red pepper flakes

1 teaspoon salt

1 teaspoon freshly ground black pepper

FOR THE SKEWERS

¾ pound large shrimp, peeled and deveined

¾ pound medium sea scallops

1 tablespoon canola oil

TO MAKE THE CHIMICHURRI SAUCE

In a food processor, combine the parsley, oregano, red onion, garlic, red wine vinegar, olive oil, red pepper flakes, salt, and black pepper. Pulse several times until combined, leaving some chunks in the mixture. Transfer to a serving bowl to allow flavors to combine.

TO MAKE THE SKEWERS

1. Meanwhile, heat a grill or stove-top grill pan to medium heat. Thread the shrimp and scallops onto skewers. (If using wooden skewers, be sure to soak in water for at least 30 minutes before using.) Brush the shrimp and scallops with canola oil and grill for about 3 minutes on each side, until they are opaque.

2. Remove from the grill or pan and place on a serving platter. Spoon chimichurri sauce over the top, reserving leftover sauce for dipping.

SERVING SUGGESTION: Pair these grilled skewers with grilled vegetables, or prepare a sheet pan to roast veggies if cooking indoors. Ideal pairings include roasted potatoes, zucchini, or cauliflower. You can also prepare with a starchy side such as orzo or rice.

PER SERVING:

Calories: 380; Total Fat: 29g; Saturated Fat: 4g; Polyunsaturated Fat: 3.5g; Monounsaturated Fat: 20g; Cholesterol: 130mg; Sodium: 860mg; Carbohydrates: 9g; Fiber: 2g; Sugars: 1g; Added Sugars: 0g; Protein: 23g

DIY SUSHI STACKS

Serves 4

PREP TIME: 10 minutes

QUICK PREP

While they're not quite sushi in the traditional sense, these stacks are the all-in-one type of meal that works well for a quick lunch or dinner. The secret is removing the bottom of a can to use as the mold for the stacks. If that's too much, this recipe is just as good in a bowl.

2 cups cooked white rice, cooled

2 tablespoons rice vinegar

½ cucumber, diced

¼ cup shredded carrots

2 scallions, thinly sliced

Juice of 1 lime

¼ cup mayonnaise

1 to 2 tablespoons Sriracha or hot chili sauce

2 (5-ounce) cans tuna, drained

Nonstick cooking spray

1 avocado, diced

1 tablespoon low-sodium soy sauce

Sesame seeds, for garnish

1. In a large bowl, mix the cooked rice with rice vinegar.

2. In a medium bowl, mix the cucumber, carrots, scallion, and lime juice. Set aside.

3. In another large bowl, mix the mayonnaise and Sriracha sauce together, then add the tuna and stir to combine.

4. To build the stacks, slightly coat the inside of a tuna can or a large ring mold with nonstick cooking spray. Place the mold in the center of a plate. Start by placing a quarter of the rice inside and gently packing down. Add a quarter each of the carrot-cucumber mixture, avocado, and then tuna. Press gently after adding each layer.

5. Carefully lift the mold, drizzle soy sauce over each stack, sprinkle with sesame seeds, and serve.

SERVING SUGGESTION: Serve with pickled ginger and wasabi. Add crumbled nori if serving in a bowl. Adjust the amount of rice or other toppings to fit your appetite.

PER SERVING:

Calories: 370; Total Fat: 14g; Saturated Fat: 2.5g; Polyunsaturated Fat: 4.5g; Monounsaturated Fat: 5.5g; Cholesterol: 40mg; Sodium: 640mg; Carbohydrates: 37g; Fiber: 3g; Sugars: 3g; Added Sugars: 0.5g; Protein: 24g

ORANGE-SESAME SEARED SCALLOPS WITH SNOW PEAS & BROCCOLI

Serves 4

PREP TIME: 10 minutes / COOK TIME: 15 minutes

`30 MINUTES`

Many sauces bring interesting, unique flavors to familiar ingredients, but they don't have to be complex or intricate. This orange-sesame sauce serves as a glaze for the seared scallops and can be used for cooked vegetables as well. Be sure to note that soy sauces, unless verified, are not gluten-free.

¼ cup honey

2 tablespoons rice vinegar

2 tablespoons orange juice

2 teaspoons red pepper flakes

2 teaspoons orange zest

2 teaspoons sesame seeds

1 teaspoon dried ginger

1 teaspoon low-sodium soy sauce

3 tablespoons sesame oil, divided

1½ pounds sea scallops (about 16 to 18 scallops)

1 pound broccoli, cut into florets

1 pound snow peas, trimmed

1 bunch scallions, chopped, for garnish

1. In a small saucepan over low heat, mix the honey, rice vinegar, orange juice, red pepper flakes, orange zest, sesame seeds, ginger, soy sauce, and 1 tablespoon of sesame oil. Once warmed, the texture should be smooth and sticky. Turn off the heat and hold warm until needed.

2. Pat the scallops dry, and heat the remaining 2 tablespoons of sesame oil over medium-high heat in a skillet. Once the oil is heated, sear the scallops for 2 minutes on each side, or until opaque and firm. Work in two batches if needed to avoid overcrowding the pan. Transfer to a paper towel–lined plate and cover to hold warm.

3. In the same skillet over high heat, sauté the broccoli and snow peas, stirring occasionally, until crisp-tender, 5 to 7 minutes. The vegetables should appear vibrant green. Reduce the heat to low, then add the scallops back into the skillet. Drizzle the sauce over the top and allow to heat through. Top with the scallions and serve immediately.

SERVING SUGGESTION: Complete your meal by pairing with rice or soba noodles. To make this a vegetarian meal, swap the scallops for firm tofu. Cut into cubes and sear over high heat in sesame oil until the edges become crispy.

PER SERVING:

Calories: 370; Total Fat: 12g; Saturated Fat: 2g; Polyunsaturated Fat: 4.5g; Monounsaturated Fat: 4g; Cholesterol: 40mg; Sodium: 770mg; Carbohydrates: 41g; Fiber: 7g; Sugars: 25g; Added Sugars: 17g; Protein: 27g

CREAMY COD PICCATA WITH SPAGHETTI SQUASH

Serves 4

PREP TIME: 5 minutes / COOK TIME: 1 hour

GLUTEN-FREE

This meal can take a little longer to prepare than other recipes in the book, so save it for a night when you're not feeling rushed. While the spaghetti squash is cooking, you'll have time to prepare the rest of the dish. I time it so that I take the spaghetti squash out of the oven as soon as I drop the cod in the pan. Letting the squash cool slightly before shredding makes it a little easier to create longer pieces.

1 large spaghetti squash (about 4 pounds)

1 tablespoon extra-virgin olive oil, plus more for brushing

Pinch salt

Pinch freshly ground black pepper

2 tablespoons butter, divided

4 (6-ounce) cod fillets

3 garlic cloves, minced

¼ cup white wine

1 cup low-sodium vegetable stock

Juice of 2 lemons

3 tablespoons capers, drained, plus more for garnish

2 teaspoons cornstarch

2 tablespoons cold water

½ cup half-and-half

Fresh parsley, for garnish

1. Preheat the oven to 400°F. Line a baking sheet with parchment paper or aluminum foil.

2. Use a very sharp knife to carefully cut the spaghetti squash in half. Scoop out the seeds. Brush with olive oil and season with salt and black pepper, then place flat-side down on the prepared baking sheet. Cover with foil and seal, then bake for 50 minutes.

3. Meanwhile, in a large nonstick skillet, heat the 1 tablespoon olive oil and 1 tablespoon of butter. Pat the cod fillets dry and place in the pan once heated. Cook for about 4 minutes on each side, or until easily flaked. Once finished, transfer to a plate and cover to hold warm.

4. In the same skillet, add the remaining 1 tablespoon of butter and the garlic. Cook for 1 minute, then add the white wine to deglaze the pan, scraping up any browned bits from the bottom. Add the vegetable stock, lemon juice, and capers, and stir.

5. In a small bowl, whisk the cornstarch and cold water together to create a slurry. Add it to the skillet, and bring to a simmer. Stir in the half-and-half and allow to thicken to a gravy-like consistency.

6. To serve, shred the spaghetti squash into noodles with a fork and divide evenly among four plates. Place the cooked cod on top, and add the sauce. Garnish with fresh parsley and additional capers.

INGREDIENT TIP: The cornstarch works best as a thickener when made into a slurry first. That's why we add cold water to the dry cornstarch and mix into a thin paste. It will appear milky and opaque. Pour it into the sauce and bring to a simmer, stirring constantly so you'll know when it starts to thicken.

PAN-SEARED TROUT WITH EDAMAME SUCCOTASH

Serves 4

PREP TIME: 10 minutes / **COOK TIME:** 15 minutes

`30 MINUTES` `GLUTEN-FREE`

A traditional succotash is made with lima beans. While you can certainly use those in this recipe, I personally like the texture that edamame brings to this dish. To thaw frozen, shelled edamame in advance, simply store in the refrigerator overnight or submerge in water before cooking.

1 tablespoon butter

1½ cups sweet corn kernels

1½ cups shelled edamame, thawed

1 zucchini, diced

1 cup halved cherry tomatoes

Pinch salt

Pinch freshly ground black pepper

6 to 8 fresh basil leaves

1 tablespoon canola oil

4 trout fillets, skin on

2 lemons, cut into wedges

1. In a large skillet, over medium-high heat, melt the butter. Add the corn, edamame, and zucchini, and cook for 3 to 5 minutes, then stir in tomatoes, salt, and pepper. Remove from the skillet and transfer to a serving bowl. Chop or chiffonade (see tip on page 64) the fresh basil, and sprinkle on top.

2. Return the pan to medium-high heat, and add the canola oil. Once heated, lay the trout, skin-side down, in the heated pan. Season the top with salt and pepper, if desired. Sear for about 6 minutes, then carefully flip the fillets and cook for 1 to 2 minutes more.

3. To serve, plate each trout fillet over a quarter of the vegetable mixture and squeeze the lemon wedges over the top.

INGREDIENT TIP: Trout with skin is often found as an intact, whole fish. If you prefer not to deal with the hassle of deboning the fillets, ask your fishmonger to do this for you. If you purchase trout as individual fillets with skin removed, be sure to use extra care when searing so as not to have them break apart in the skillet.

PER SERVING:

Calories: 460; Total Fat: 24g; Saturated Fat: 6g; Polyunsaturated Fat: 5g; Monounsaturated Fat: 10g; Cholesterol: 115mg; Sodium: 290mg; Carbohydrates: 19g; Fiber: 5g; Sugars: 5g; Added Sugars: 0g; Protein: 44g

BROILED WHITEFISH WITH ORZO RISOTTO

Serves 4

PREP TIME: 5 minutes / COOK TIME: 20 minutes

30 MINUTES

Risotto typically takes a long time to prepare, but this version speeds up the process so you can deliver dinner to the table in less than 30 minutes. If you want to infuse more flavor into your dish, try preparing it with a low-sodium vegetable or seafood stock instead of water.

Nonstick cooking spray (optional)

4 (4-ounce) whitefish fillets

1 tablespoon Italian seasoning

1 tablespoon extra-virgin olive oil

1⅓ cups uncooked orzo pasta

3½ cups water

3 garlic cloves, minced

2 cups cherry tomatoes, quartered

1 tablespoon capers, drained and rinsed, plus more for garnish

1 teaspoon salt

1 teaspoon freshly ground black pepper

1 tablespoon butter

1 tablespoon fresh parsley, chopped

1. Position the top oven rack 6 to 8 inches from the heating element. Preheat the oven to broil for at least 10 minutes.

2. Prepare a baking sheet with nonstick cooking spray. Evenly space the fillets on top and coat with the Italian seasoning, saving the excess. Broil until the fish is fully cooked and easily flaked, 8 to 10 minutes. Remove from the oven. Tent with foil to keep warm while the orzo finishes cooking.

3. Meanwhile, in a large skillet over medium heat, toast the orzo until the color becomes a light golden brown, about 2 minutes. Add the water and bring to a simmer. Stir frequently. Once most of the liquid is absorbed, after about 15 minutes, add the garlic, cherry tomatoes, capers, remaining Italian seasoning, salt, and black pepper. Continue cooking until all liquid is absorbed. Remove from the heat, and stir in the butter.

4. Plate a quarter of the orzo risotto and top with one fillet. Garnish with the parsley and additional capers, repeat with the remaining orzo risotto and fish, and serve.

INGREDIENT TIP: Whitefish refers to multiple species of nonoily fish. Commonly found varieties include cod, halibut, and tilapia, any of which would work well in this recipe.

PER SERVING:

Calories: 420; Total Fat: 15g; Saturated Fat: 3.5g; Polyunsaturated Fat: 3g; Monounsaturated Fat: 5.5g; Cholesterol: 75mg; Sodium: 180mg; Carbohydrates: 44g; Fiber: 7g; Sugars: 3g; Added Sugars: 0g; Protein: 28g

DIJON WALNUT-CRUSTED FISH

Serves 4

PREP TIME: 10 minutes / COOK TIME: 15 minutes

30 MINUTES

Whitefish such as halibut, cod, mahi-mahi, or tilapia are great introductions to fish recipes because they are less fishy than other species. For those who still aren't fully convinced, I recommend using a flavorful breading like this Dijon mustard and walnut combination.

2 large eggs

1 cup panko bread crumbs

¾ cup finely chopped walnuts

½ cup grated Parmesan cheese

2 tablespoons melted butter

1½ tablespoons Dijon mustard

1 tablespoon Italian seasoning

Pinch salt

Pinch freshly ground black pepper

4 (6-ounce) whitefish fillets, skin removed, patted dry

1. Preheat the oven to 425°F. Line a baking sheet with parchment paper or aluminum foil.

2. In a medium bowl, lightly beat the eggs to form a simple egg wash. In a large bowl, mix to combine the bread crumbs, walnuts, cheese, butter, Dijon mustard, Italian seasoning, salt, and black pepper for the crust, and place next to the egg wash. The texture should resemble moist crumbles. Dip the fillets into the egg wash, then coat with the crust mixture and place on the baking sheet.

3. Bake for 10 to 12 minutes, or until fully cooked and easily flaked. The crust should appear golden brown and crispy. Serve immediately.

SERVING SUGGESTION: Pair this recipe with a simple side salad or roasted vegetables to complete your meal.

PER SERVING:

Calories: 570; Total Fat: 37g; Saturated Fat: 9g; Polyunsaturated Fat: 15g; Monounsaturated Fat: 9.5g; Cholesterol: 175mg; Sodium: 440mg; Carbohydrates: 16g; Fiber: 2g; Sugars: 2g; Added Sugars: <1g; Protein: 44g

NO-COOK SHRIMP CEVICHE

Serves 4

PREP TIME: 10 minutes, plus 20 minutes to chill

`30 MINUTES` `GLUTEN-FREE`

Ceviche is common on the coasts, where raw shrimp or fish are plentiful, because no cooking is required. The acid from the fruit helps to "cook" the seafood. If you're farther from the coasts, I recommend starting with precooked shrimp, not only to speed up the process but also for food safety measures.

1 pound precooked shrimp,
finely chopped

½ red onion, finely diced

1 small jalapeño, minced

1 garlic clove, minced

1½ cups freshly squeezed lime juice

½ cup pineapple juice

½ cup chopped fresh cilantro

1 large tomato, diced

½ cup diced pineapple

1 avocado, diced

Pinch salt

Pinch freshly ground black pepper

1. In a large bowl, combine the shrimp, red onion, jalapeño, garlic, lime juice, and pineapple juice. Stir to combine, then cover and place in the refrigerator to chill for 20 minutes.

2. Remove the shrimp mixture from the refrigerator and strain, reserving the excess liquid in a measuring cup. Add the cilantro, tomato, pineapple, and avocado to the shrimp mixture. Stir to combine, then add about 2 tablespoons of the reserved liquid back into the mixture.

3. Season with salt and black pepper and serve chilled.

SERVING SUGGESTION: Serve with tortilla chips or on top of salad greens. You can also add this mixture to a bowl with prepared rice and black beans.

PER SERVING:

Calories: 170; Total Fat: 7g; Saturated Fat: 1g; Polyunsaturated Fat: 1g; Monounsaturated Fat: 3.5g; Cholesterol: 145mg; Sodium: 650mg; Carbohydrates: 12g; Fiber: 4g; Sugars: 5g; Added Sugars: 0g; Protein: 17g

BAKED SALMON WITH GREEK VEGGIES & AVOCADO TZATZIKI

Serves 4

PREP TIME: 10 minutes / COOK TIME: 15 minutes

`30 MINUTES` `GLUTEN-FREE`

My husband comes from a large Greek family, and I remember the first time I tried authentic feta cheese. I was shocked by how different it was from the crumbled versions I'd tasted in the past. Now, we rely on the blocks of fresh feta packed in water for the best taste and quality, but don't worry because the drier, crumbled versions also work well in this recipe.

4 (6-ounce) salmon fillets

1 tablespoon extra-virgin olive oil, plus more for brushing

Pinch salt

Freshly ground black pepper

1 avocado

½ cup plain, low-fat Greek yogurt

1 tablespoon fresh dill, chopped

Juice of 1 lemon

½ teaspoon garlic powder

1½ cups shredded cucumber

2 cups cucumber, sliced

1 cup halved cherry tomatoes

½ red onion, thinly sliced

12 to 16 Kalamata olives, pitted

1 tablespoon balsamic vinegar

1 teaspoon dried oregano

½ cup feta cheese crumbles

1. Preheat the oven to 400°F. Line a baking sheet with parchment paper or aluminum foil.

2. Pat the salmon fillets dry, brush with olive oil, and season with salt and pepper. Place on the baking sheet and bake for 10 to 12 minutes, or until easily flaked with a fork.

3. Meanwhile, in a small bowl, make the tzatziki. Mash the avocado until creamy and smooth. Add the Greek yogurt, dill, lemon juice, garlic powder, and shredded cucumber, season with pepper, and mix well. Cover and chill until ready to serve.

4. In a large bowl, mix to combine the sliced cucumber, cherry tomatoes, onion, and Kalamata olives. Drizzle with 1 tablespoon of olive oil and balsamic vinegar. Sprinkle with the oregano, and top with the feta cheese.

5. When the salmon is finished cooking, remove from the oven and place on four plates. Top with the avocado tzatziki or serve on the side. Evenly divide the Greek veggies onto each plate and serve immediately.

SERVING SUGGESTION: This mixture of dressed veggies can easily become an entrée salad. Add a hefty handful of your favorite salad greens plus additional raw veggies like bell peppers or zucchini. Add additional dressing, if needed, and top with your favorite protein.

GOUDA TUNA NOODLE CASSEROLE

Serves 6

PREP TIME: 25 minutes / COOK TIME: 35 minutes

Wintery weather seems to induce a craving for comfort foods. The inspiration for this recipe came from the days of making tuna noodle casserole in a stove-top skillet. This version, which bakes in savory, umami flavors, is worth the wait.

4 tablespoons butter, divided

1 yellow onion, diced

1 (8-ounce) package white or baby bella mushrooms, sliced

3 tablespoons low-sodium soy sauce

2 tablespoons apple cider vinegar

12 ounces rotini pasta

¼ cup all-purpose flour

2 cups low-sodium vegetable stock

½ cup heavy (whipping) cream

1½ cups frozen green peas, thawed

2 (5-ounce) cans tuna, drained

1½ cups shredded Gouda cheese

¾ cup panko bread crumbs

1. Preheat the oven to 350°F.

2. In a large skillet over medium-high heat, heat 1 tablespoon of butter Add the onion, and sauté for 3 to 5 minutes. Add the mushrooms, and cook for 2 to 3 minutes more. Add the soy sauce and apple cider vinegar, and continue cooking until the liquid is reduced almost completely, about 7 minutes. Remove the mixture from the skillet and set aside.

3. Bring a medium saucepan of water to a boil. Cook the pasta according to package instructions. Then drain, transfer to a large bowl, and set aside.

4. In the same skillet over medium heat, melt the remaining 3 tablespoons of butter. Immediately add the flour, and stir to combine to form a simple roux. Continue cooking, stirring frequently, until the roux becomes a golden brown. Add the stock and cream. Bring to a simmer, stirring to prevent scalding. Once the mixture has thickened to a gravy consistency, remove from the heat and pour over the pasta.

5. Add the peas, tuna, and sauce to the pasta, and stir well to combine. Transfer to a large, lightly greased casserole dish or baking dish. Top with the Gouda cheese, then sprinkle the panko bread crumbs over the cheese. Bake, covered, for 20 to 25 minutes, or until the cheese is bubbling and the topping becomes slightly browned. Allow to cool slightly, and serve hot.

INGREDIENT TIP: While cooking, the mushrooms and onions will release additional liquid. Adjust cooking time as needed, or sauté over slightly higher heat, uncovered. To save time, the pasta may be cooked at the same time as the mushrooms and onions.

PER SERVING:

Calories: 580; Total Fat: 23g; Saturated Fat: 13g; Polyunsaturated Fat: 1.5g; Monounsaturated Fat: 5.5g; Cholesterol: 90mg; Sodium: 910mg; Carbohydrates: 61g; Fiber: 9g; Sugars: 7g; Added Sugars: 0g; Protein: 33g

SEAFOOD SALAD-STUFFED AVOCADOS

Serves 4

PREP TIME: 10 minutes

QUICK PREP GLUTEN-FREE

I grew up eating the prepared seafood salad from the deli section of our small-town grocery store. As I grew older, I started craving those familiar flavors but wanted to replicate it in an easy homemade recipe. This version is served in an avocado, but I still enjoy it served with crackers and crunchy vegetables for dipping.

¼ pound precooked shrimp, cooled and finely chopped

¼ cup crabmeat, flaked

1 scallion, thinly sliced

2 tablespoons chopped fresh parsley

1 tablespoon hot sauce or Sriracha

1 teaspoon Dijon mustard

2 tablespoons plain, low-fat Greek yogurt

1 tablespoon mayonnaise

½ teaspoon Old Bay seasoning

1 teaspoon lemon zest

Juice of 1 lemon

4 avocados

1. In a large bowl, stir to combine the shrimp, crabmeat, scallion, and parsley.

2. In a small bowl, prepare the dressing by combining the hot sauce, Dijon mustard, Greek yogurt, mayonnaise, Old Bay, lemon zest, and lemon juice, stirring until smooth.

3. Halve each avocado, and remove the pit. Use a spoon to remove more of the flesh, leaving about half to three-quarters of an inch inside the peel. Add that avocado flesh to the dressing mixture, stirring it in.

4. Scoop the seafood mixture into each avocado half and serve immediately.

SUBSTITUTION: While imitation crabmeat can be an appropriate stand-in, you may prefer to swap the crabmeat for additional shrimp or another type of prepared seafood if the crabmeat is difficult to find or too expensive.

PER SERVING:

Calories: 330; Total Fat: 24g; Saturated Fat: 3.5g; Polyunsaturated Fat: 4g; Monounsaturated Fat: 14g; Cholesterol: 75mg; Sodium: 240mg; Carbohydrates: 16g; Fiber: 9g; Sugars: 3g; Added Sugars: 0g; Protein: 16g

Roasted Carrots with Zesty Gremolata & Pistachios, page 127

SIDES & SNACKS

SPICED TABBOULEH WITH CHICKPEAS

Serves 4

PREP TIME: 5 minutes / COOK TIME: 30 minutes

VEGETARIAN

This traditional Middle Eastern salad features bulgur, parsley, mint, and lemon. This version includes chickpeas to boost the fiber content and a variety of spices to create a full-flavored side dish to accompany your main entrée. Be sure to use bulgur instead of bulgur wheat to keep the cooking time short.

2 cups water

½ cup bulgur

1 large English cucumber, cut into ¼-inch cubes

1 Roma tomato, seeded and chopped

2 scallions, thinly sliced

1¼ cups chopped fresh flat-leaf parsley

½ cup chopped fresh mint

1½ teaspoons lemon zest

¼ teaspoon salt, plus more to taste

¼ teaspoon ground cinnamon

¼ teaspoon ground allspice

⅛ teaspoon ground cayenne pepper

1 (14.5-ounce) can chickpeas, drained and rinsed

Juice of 1 lemon

2 tablespoons extra-virgin olive oil

1. In a medium saucepan over high heat, bring the water to a boil. Once boiling, add the bulgur and remove from the heat. Let sit, uncovered, for 20 to 30 minutes, until tender, then drain any excess liquid using a fine-mesh strainer.

2. In a large bowl, combine the cucumber, tomato, scallions, parsley, mint, lemon zest, salt, cinnamon, allspice, and cayenne pepper.

3. Add the bulgur and chickpeas to the bowl.

4. In a small measuring cup, whisk together the lemon juice and olive oil, then pour over the tabbouleh mixture. Gently fold to combine. Serve immediately or allow to chill for 30 to 60 minutes before serving. Store leftovers in the refrigerator for up to 5 days.

INGREDIENT TIP: To avoid a bitter flavor, remove the parsley leaves from the stems before chopping.

PER SERVING:

Calories: 230; Total Fat: 9g; Saturated Fat: 1g; Polyunsaturated Fat: 1.5g; Monounsaturated Fat: 5.5g; Cholesterol: 0mg; Sodium: 320mg; Carbohydrates: 34mg; Fiber: 9g; Sugars: 5g; Added Sugars: 0g; Protein: 8g

GRILLED VEGETABLE PLATTER WITH DIY HONEY-MUSTARD DRESSING

Serves 6

PREP TIME: 10 minutes / COOK TIME: 15 minutes

30 MINUTES GLUTEN-FREE VEGETARIAN

Grilling season is one of my favorite times of the year, but it's not always practical when the weather doesn't cooperate. I like to bring that grilled flavor to cold-weather meals by preparing veggies on a well-seasoned grill pan. This dish features a tangy honey-mustard dressing.

FOR THE GRILLED VEGETABLE PLATTER

2 red bell peppers, cut into thick slices

2 large portobello caps

1 medium eggplant, cut lengthwise into ¼- to ½-inch slices

1 large sweet potato, peeled and cut lengthwise into ¼-inch slices

½ head cauliflower, cut into large florets

¼ cup extra-virgin olive oil

Pinch salt

Pinch freshly ground black pepper

3 cups salad greens, loosely packed

FOR THE DRESSING

½ cup extra-virgin olive oil

¼ cup white vinegar

2 teaspoons Dijon mustard

2 teaspoons honey

½ teaspoon garlic powder

Pinch salt

Pinch freshly ground black pepper

TO MAKE THE GRILLED VEGETABLES

1. If grilling outside, bring your grill to medium heat. If using an indoor grill pan, use the stove-top burner to bring the pan to medium-high heat.

2. Brush the red bell peppers, portobello caps, eggplant, sweet potato, and cauliflower with the olive oil, and season lightly with salt and pepper. Place on the preheated grill surface and cook for 10 to 15 minutes, until tender, flipping about halfway through. The eggplant, sweet potato, and cauliflower may have longer cooking times depending on their thickness.

continued

TO MAKE THE DRESSING AND SERVE

1. In a small mason jar or container with a lid, combine the olive oil, vinegar, Dijon mustard, honey, garlic powder, salt, and pepper. Seal and shake until the ingredients are well mixed. Serve immediately or store in the fridge for up to 3 to 4 days.

2. Arrange the salad greens on a large serving platter. Remove the veggies from the grill and place on top of the greens. Lightly drizzle with the dressing and serve warm.

INGREDIENT TIP: Be sure to leave all the pieces large enough to prevent them from falling through the grill grates. If needed, use a grill basket or roast veggies in the oven instead.

PER SERVING:

Calories: 240; Total Fat: 17g; Saturated Fat: 2.5g; Polyunsaturated Fat: 2g; Monounsaturated Fat: 12g; Cholesterol: 0mg; Sodium: 115g; Carbohydrates: 21g; Fiber: 7g; Sugars: 11g; Added Sugars: 2g; Protein: 4g

ROASTED CARROTS WITH ZESTY GREMOLATA & PISTACHIOS

Serves 4

PREP TIME: 10 minutes / COOK TIME: 20 minutes

30 MINUTES GLUTEN-FREE VEGETARIAN

This recipe was born from my desire to create less food waste. My favorite vendors at the farmers' market sell carrots with the greens still attached, and I wanted to find a way to use them. A gremolata is a simple condiment to season grilled fish, roasted vegetables, and more and can help you use up any leftover herbs or citrus.

12 carrots with greens
1 shallot, thinly sliced
2 garlic cloves, minced
1 tablespoon extra-virgin olive oil
1 teaspoon ground cumin
1 teaspoon chili powder
Pinch salt
Pinch freshly ground black pepper
Juice and zest of 1 lemon, divided
¼ cup chopped fresh cilantro
½ jalapeño pepper, minced
¼ cup pistachios, finely chopped

1. Preheat the oven to 400°F.

2. Remove the carrot greens and set aside, then wash, trim, and peel the carrots, if you like. If needed, halve larger carrots for even roasting. In a large bowl, toss the carrots with the shallot, garlic, olive oil, cumin, chili powder, salt, and pepper. Arrange in a single layer on a baking sheet. Drizzle with half of the lemon juice. Roast for 20 minutes, or until the carrots are tender, flipping once.

3. Meanwhile, to make the gremolata, wash and dry the carrot greens. Coarsely chop to yield ¼ cup, then, in a mixing bowl, mix together with the cilantro, jalapeño pepper, the remaining lemon juice, and 1 tablespoon of lemon zest. When the carrots are done roasting, transfer to a serving platter and top with the gremolata. Top with the pistachios and serve immediately.

VARIATION: If using bagged carrots, substitute parsley for the greens. The classic gremolata recipe can also be made with anchovy paste; if you'd like to change the flavor, add 1 to 2 teaspoons and adjust as needed.

PER SERVING:

Calories: 160; Total Fat: 8g; Saturated Fat: 1g; Polyunsaturated Fat: 1.5g; Monounsaturated Fat: 4.5g; Cholesterol: 0mg; Sodium: 250mg; Carbohydrates: 23g; Fiber: 7g; Sugars: 10g; Added Sugars: 0g; Protein: 4g

RED CHILE-GLAZED BUTTERNUT SQUASH

Serves 6

PREP TIME: 10 minutes / COOK TIME: 25 minutes

GLUTEN-FREE VEGETARIAN

When my dad was growing up, his family would choose one type of vegetable and plant rows and rows of it in their garden. He still does this, and after his recent planting blitz, I found myself with an abundance of butternut squash. After eating it a few times in a row, I was craving a new way to prepare it. This sweet and spicy glaze is now one of our favorite ways to enjoy this squash, but it pairs well with many other vegetables, too.

¼ cup extra-virgin olive oil

Juice of 1 orange

1 teaspoon honey

1 teaspoon apple cider vinegar

½ tablespoon red pepper flakes, plus more for garnish (optional)

2 garlic cloves, minced

½ tablespoon dried thyme

Pinch salt

Pinch freshly ground black pepper

1 large butternut squash

1. Preheat the oven to 400°F.

2. In a small bowl, mix together the olive oil, orange juice, honey, vinegar, red pepper flakes, garlic, thyme, salt, and pepper to let flavors combine.

3. Meanwhile, carefully use a very sharp knife to halve the squash lengthwise. Scoop out the seeds. Place the squash flat-side down and slice into ¼-inch to ½-inch half-moon shapes. Place in a large mixing bowl.

4. Line a baking sheet with parchment paper or aluminum foil. Pour the glaze over the squash, toss to combine, then arrange on the baking sheet in a single layer. Use a second baking sheet if needed to avoid stacking pieces.

5. Roast for 12 minutes, then flip and roast for 10 to 12 minutes more, until the edges begin to brown and the squash is fully cooked. Garnish with additional red pepper flakes, if desired, and serve hot.

INGREDIENT TIP: Slicing a butternut squash is no easy task, so if you prefer to purchase ready-to-cook squash, look for cubes or slices in the prepared foods section of your grocery store.

PER SERVING:

Calories: 130; Total Fat: 9g; Saturated Fat: 1.5g; Polyunsaturated Fat: 1g; Monounsaturated Fat: 6.5g; Cholesterol: 0mg; Sodium: 30mg; Carbohydrates: 14g; Fiber: 2g; Sugars: 4g; Added Sugars: 1g; Protein: 1g

ISRAELI COUSCOUS WITH PEARS & GORGONZOLA

Serves 6

PREP TIME: 5 minutes / COOK TIME: 10 minutes

30 MINUTES   VEGETARIAN

The flavor combination of sweet with savory or salty never seems to get old for me. The pears and dried cranberries offer up the sweet, then the Gorgonzola comes through with the rest. If you're not a fan, you can swap for goat cheese or feta to suit your tastes.

1½ cups water

1 cup uncooked pearled Israeli couscous

¼ teaspoon salt, plus more to taste

⅓ cup extra-virgin olive oil

2½ tablespoons balsamic vinegar

4 cups spinach, thinly sliced

1 (15-ounce) can pears, drained and diced

¾ cup chopped walnuts

¾ cup dried cranberries

¾ cup Gorgonzola cheese crumbles

Freshly ground black pepper

1. In a medium saucepan over high heat, bring the water to a boil. Add the couscous and salt. Reduce the heat to medium and simmer, uncovered, for 6 to 8 minutes, or until most liquid is absorbed. Remove from the heat and allow to stand, uncovered, to cool as you prepare the other ingredients.

2. In a small measuring cup, whisk the olive oil and vinegar to combine. Set aside.

3. In a large bowl, combine the spinach, pears, walnuts, and dried cranberries. Fold together gently while adding the cooled couscous.

4. Drizzle the balsamic dressing over the top, and add the Gorgonzola cheese crumbles. Gently stir to combine. Season with salt and pepper to taste, and serve immediately or chill for up to 30 minutes.

LEFTOVERS: This dish will store well in the fridge for up to 5 days if left undressed. If planning for leftovers, mix small batches of dressing before serving or store separately.

PER SERVING:

Calories: 420; Total Fat: 26g; Saturated Fat: 6g; Polyunsaturated Fat: 8g; Monounsaturated Fat: 10g; Cholesterol: 15mg; Sodium: 310mg; Carbohydrates: 42g; Fiber: 5g; Sugars: 15g; Added Sugars: 6g; Protein: 9g

CONFETTI QUINOA WITH HONEY-LIME DRESSING

Serves 6

PREP TIME: 5 minutes / COOK TIME: 20 minutes

30 MINUTES **GLUTEN-FREE** **VEGETARIAN**

When I first started making this recipe, I used it as a simple side that packed great for leftovers. But as soon as I brought it to a potluck, it became one of my most requested recipes. It's also a favorite, because you can swap ingredients to make it your own.

FOR THE QUINOA

3 cups water

1½ cups uncooked quinoa

Pinch salt

1 red bell pepper

1 orange bell pepper

1 green bell pepper

1 cup sweet corn kernels, canned or frozen

1 small red onion, diced

1 (15.5-ounce) can black beans, drained and rinsed

½ cup chopped fresh cilantro

FOR THE DRESSING

3 tablespoons extra-virgin olive oil

Juice of 2 limes

½ tablespoon honey

2 garlic cloves, minced

1 teaspoon ground cumin

½ teaspoon chili powder

Pinch salt

Pinch freshly ground black pepper

TO MAKE THE QUINOA

1. In a medium saucepan over high heat, bring the water to a boil. Add the quinoa and salt. Reduce to a simmer and cook, uncovered, for 15 to 20 minutes, or until all liquid is absorbed. Remove from the heat and fluff with a fork.

2. Meanwhile, dice the bell peppers. Add them to a large bowl with the corn, onion, black beans, and cilantro. Toss to combine. When the quinoa has cooled, add to the bowl and mix well.

TO MAKE THE DRESSING AND SERVE

1. In a small measuring cup, whisk the olive oil, lime juice, honey, garlic, cumin, chili powder, salt, and pepper. Adjust flavor as needed. Pour over the quinoa mixture and fold together until the dressing is evenly distributed.

2. Serve immediately, or store in the refrigerator for 3 to 5 days. May be served warm or chilled.

SERVING SUGGESTION: Prepare a larger batch of the dressing and store separately. Use it as a dressing for salads or a simple marinade for your favorite proteins.

PER SERVING:

Calories: 320; Total Fat: 10g; Saturated Fat: 1.5g; Polyunsaturated Fat: 2.5g; Monounsaturated Fat: 6g; Cholesterol: 0mg; Sodium: 130mg; Carbohydrates: 48g; Fiber: 9g; Sugars: 7g; Added Sugars: 2g; Protein: 11g

SLATHERED APPLE SNACKERS

Serves 1

PREP TIME: 5 minutes

QUICK PREP GLUTEN-FREE VEGETARIAN

These were coined "apple donuts" in my household the first time I made them. While there's a special place in my heart for actual donuts, I find that apples and nut butters are a reliable snack combo that can keep me satisfied until my next meal. I like to mix up the toppings, but this version highlights crunch and sweetness for a satisfying snack or dessert.

1 Granny Smith apple

1½ tablespoons creamy peanut butter

½ tablespoon hemp hearts

1 tablespoon mini chocolate chips

2 tablespoons dried cranberries or raisins

1. Lay the apple on its side and slice into ½-inch-thick rounds. Lay the rounds flat, and use the mouth of a bottle or a spoon to remove the core from the center.

2. Use a butter knife or spoon to spread peanut butter onto each slice. Top with the hemp hearts, chocolate chips, and cranberries, distributing evenly over each slice. Serve immediately.

VARIATION: Try this snack with other varieties of apples or nut butters. You can also swap out the peanut butter for vanilla yogurt or Nutella and mix up your toppings to include nuts, seeds, or your favorite dried fruit.

PER SERVING:

Calories: 340; Total Fat: 17g; Saturated Fat: 4g; Polyunsaturated Fat: 5g; Monounsaturated Fat: 6g; Cholesterol: 0mg; Sodium: 110mg; Carbohydrates: 45g; Fiber: 8g; Sugars: 32g; Added Sugars: 10g; Protein: 9g

CURRY TUNA SALAD SNACKERS

Serves 4

PREP TIME: 10 minutes

QUICK PREP GLUTEN-FREE

I love to peruse the spice section and specialized spice markets. It seems I always end up with an abundance of curry powder due to my excitement. I was searching for other ways to use this vibrant, flavorful spice blend and landed on tuna salad. This variation is served with crunchy cucumbers but can also be paired with other raw vegetables, your favorite crackers, or tortilla chips.

¼ cup plain, low-fat Greek yogurt

1 tablespoon mayonnaise

1 teaspoon curry powder

¼ teaspoon red pepper flakes

1 teaspoon freshly squeezed lemon juice

1 (5-ounce) can tuna, drained

½ cup diced celery

¼ cup shredded carrots

¼ cup diced red onion

¼ cup chopped dried apricots

¼ cup chopped pistachios

1 large cucumber, sliced

1. In a large bowl, mix the yogurt, mayonnaise, curry powder, red pepper flakes, and lemon juice together.

2. Add the tuna, celery, carrots, red onion, dried apricots, and pistachios to the mixture, and stir to combine and evenly distribute all ingredients.

3. On a serving platter, arrange the sliced cucumbers and scoop the tuna mixture onto each one. Serve immediately or store the mixture and sliced cucumber separately for up to 3 days.

INGREDIENT TIP: Curry powders come in a variety of flavor profiles. Some carry more sweetness or spice than others, so depending on what you have available, be sure to adjust the seasoning to fit your preferences.

PER SERVING:

Calories: 170; Total Fat: 6g; Saturated Fat: 1g; Polyunsaturated Fat: 2.5g; Monounsaturated Fat: 2.5g; Cholesterol: 20mg; Sodium: 220mg; Carbohydrates: 15g; Fiber: 3g; Sugars: 9g; Added Sugars: 0g; Protein: 15g

EDAMAME-AVOCADO HUMMUS

Serves 4

PREP TIME: 10 minutes

QUICK PREP GLUTEN-FREE VEGETARIAN

My food processor is one of my most reliable kitchen appliances because it can be used for so many purposes. Whipping up a quick snack like this one is just one of them. Keep a spatula nearby so you can scrape the sides of the food processor. This will ensure that everything blends together and you get the perfect smooth texture.

1 avocado

1½ cups frozen shelled
edamame, thawed

¼ cup chopped fresh cilantro

1 scallion, cut into short pieces

1 teaspoon onion powder

2 tablespoons extra-virgin olive oil

1 tablespoon tahini

Pinch salt

Pinch freshly ground black pepper

In the bowl of your food processor, combine the avocado, edamame, cilantro, scallion, onion powder, olive oil, tahini, salt, and pepper. Pulse until the mixture starts to combine, then mix at a high speed until the mixture is smooth.

SERVING SUGGESTION: Serve with crunchy raw veggies such as carrots, sliced bell peppers, celery, radishes, or sugar snap peas. It also can be paired with your favorite crackers or pretzels.

PER SERVING:

Calories: 210; Total Fat: 17g; Saturated Fat: 2.5g; Polyunsaturated Fat: 3.5g; Monounsaturated Fat: 10g; Cholesterol: 0mg; Sodium: 50mg; Carbohydrates: 10g; Fiber: 6g; Sugars: 2g; Added Sugars: 0g; Protein: 8g

SMOKED SALMON DEVILED EGGS

Serves 4

PREP TIME: 10 minutes

QUICK PREP GLUTEN-FREE

I only started enjoying deviled eggs when I learned how to create a firmer, less runny filling, but I became a deviled egg convert after trying them with smoked salmon. Now I use cream cheese and smoked salmon to make a savory, salty snack that keeps me full between meals. They're also great for entertaining or cookouts!

6 large hard-boiled eggs

2 ounces low-fat cream cheese

2 tablespoons mayonnaise

½ teaspoon dried dill

¼ teaspoon mustard powder

Pinch salt

Pinch freshly ground black pepper

2 ounces smoked salmon

Smoked paprika, for garnish (optional)

Fresh dill, for garnish (optional)

1. Halve each egg lengthwise. Remove the yolks and add to a mixing bowl with the cream cheese, mayonnaise, dill, mustard powder, salt, and pepper. Use a fork to mash into a smooth mixture, combining until creamy with no chunks remaining.

2. Spoon the mixture into a zip-top bag and snip a bottom tip off the bag with kitchen shears. Pipe the filling back into the well of each egg white.

3. Flake the smoked salmon apart and layer on top. Garnish with smoked paprika or fresh dill, if desired, and serve.

VARIATION: This recipe also works well with smoked oysters. Drain and chop the oysters into small pieces and mix into the yolk filling, using more or less to your taste.

PER SERVING (3 DEVILED EGGS):

Calories: 160; Total Fat: 11g; Saturated Fat: 3.5g; Polyunsaturated Fat: 3g; Monounsaturated Fat: 4g; Cholesterol: 285mg; Sodium: 370mg; Carbohydrates: 3g; Fiber: 0g; Sugars: 1g; Added Sugars: 0g; Protein: 11g

NO-BAKE FRUIT & SEED GRANOLA BARS

Makes 12 bars

PREP TIME: 10 minutes, plus 30 minutes to set

GLUTEN-FREE VEGETARIAN

These granola bars are chewy with a bit of crunch thanks to the crisped rice cereal and pepitas. Pepitas are shelled pumpkin seeds and can often be found in the bulk section of your grocery store.

1½ cups uncooked rolled oats

¾ cup crisped rice cereal

¼ cup mini chocolate chips

¼ cup pepitas

¼ cup ground flaxseed

⅓ cup dried cranberries

2 tablespoons unsweetened coconut flakes

½ teaspoon ground cinnamon

¼ teaspoon salt

½ cup brown rice syrup

¼ cup creamy peanut butter

1 teaspoon vanilla extract

1. Line a 9-inch-square baking pan with parchment paper. Leave about 1 inch overhanging the edges for easy removal.

2. In a large mixing bowl, combine the oats, crisped rice, chocolate chips, pepitas, flaxseed, cranberries, coconut, cinnamon, and salt.

3. In a small saucepan over low heat, heat the brown rice syrup. Add the peanut butter, and stir until smooth. When the mixture is warm and runny, remove from the heat and add the vanilla. Stir to combine.

4. Pour the syrup mixture over the dry ingredients. Combine until all the ingredients are coated and a sticky mixture forms.

5. Scoop the mixture into the prepared pan and spread evenly. Use the back of a spatula or clean, moist hands to press into an even layer. The more tightly packed, the better the bars will hold together.

6. Place the pan in the fridge, uncovered, for at least 30 minutes to set. Remove by pulling upward on the parchment paper and transfer to a cutting board. Slice into 12 even bars.

7. Store in an airtight container in the refrigerator with a single sheet of parchment or wax paper between layers for up to 1 week. Store in the freezer by individually wrapping each bar and placing in a freezer-safe sealed bag. Thaw overnight in the fridge.

SUBSTITUTION: Swap peanut butter for almond or another nut butter for an allergen-friendly bar.

PER SERVING (1 BAR):

Calories: 170; Total Fat: 6g; Saturated Fat: 1.5g; Polyunsaturated Fat: 1.5g; Monounsaturated Fat: 1.5g; Cholesterol: 0mg; Sodium: 105mg; Carbohydrates: 24g; Fiber: 3g; Sugars: 10g; Added Sugars: 8.5g; Protein: 4g

SMOKY SWEET POTATO DIP

Serves 6

PREP TIME: 10 minutes / COOK TIME: 30 minutes

`GLUTEN-FREE` `VEGETARIAN`

If you're familiar with hummus, you'll recognize familiar ingredients in this recipe but with a unique sweet potato twist. Look for tahini in the shopping section with peanut butter and other nut butters.

2 sweet potatoes, peeled and cut into ½-inch cubes

3 garlic cloves, peeled

¼ cup plus 1 tablespoon extra-virgin olive oil, divided

⅜ teaspoon salt, divided

1 (14.5-ounce) can chickpeas, drained, liquid reserved

¼ cup tahini

Juice of 1 lemon

½ teaspoon ground cumin

½ teaspoon ground cayenne pepper

½ teaspoon smoked paprika

Crackers, pretzels, or raw vegetables, for serving

1. Preheat the oven to 400°F. Line a baking sheet with parchment paper or aluminum foil and set aside.

2. Arrange the sweet potatoes in a single layer on the prepared baking sheet. Add the garlic, then drizzle with 1 tablespoon of olive oil. Season with ⅛ teaspoon of salt.

3. Bake for 25 to 30 minutes, or until the edges of the sweet potatoes begin to brown. Remove from the oven and allow to cool for 5 minutes.

4. In the bowl of a food processor, combine the drained chickpeas and the remaining ¼ cup of olive oil, tahini, lemon juice, remaining ¼ teaspoon of salt, cumin, cayenne pepper, and smoked paprika. Pulse several times, until the ingredients start to combine.

5. Add the sweet potatoes and garlic to the food processor and continue processing until a smooth texture forms, about 60 seconds, pausing to scrape the sides of the bowl as needed. If the texture remains too thick, add the reserved liquid from the chickpeas, 1 tablespoon at a time, until desired texture is achieved.

6. Transfer from the food processor to a serving bowl and serve with crackers, pretzels, or raw vegetables.

LEFTOVERS: Store for up to 5 days in the refrigerator. Use as a spread for sandwiches or wraps, or combine with greens, veggies, and your favorite protein for a complete meal in a bowl.

PER SERVING:

Calories: 230; Total Fat: 15g; Saturated Fat: 2g; Polyunsaturated Fat: 3g; Monounsaturated Fat: 8g; Cholesterol: 0mg; Sodium: 280mg; Carbohydrates: 21g; Fiber: 5g; Sugars: 2g; Added Sugars: 4g; Protein: 5g

Easy Mango Sorbet, page 142

DESSERTS

BLUEBERRY-VANILLA CRUMBLE

Serves 12

PREP TIME: 10 minutes / COOK TIME: 40 minutes

VEGETARIAN

This vegan dessert is simple to prepare and one of my favorite dishes for potlucks and family gatherings. When I bring home leftovers, it sometimes doubles as a breakfast option with chopped nuts or more fresh fruit.

¾ cup coconut oil, plus more for coating the pan

1 cup whole-wheat flour

2 cups uncooked quick or rolled oats

½ cup tightly packed brown sugar

½ cup hemp hearts

1½ teaspoons lemon zest

1 teaspoon ground cinnamon

½ teaspoon ground nutmeg

½ teaspoon salt

1 teaspoon vanilla extract

3½ cups fresh blueberries, rinsed

1. Preheat the oven to 375°F. Line a 9-inch square baking pan with parchment paper or coat with coconut oil.

2. In a large mixing bowl, combine the flour, oats, sugar, hemp hearts, lemon zest, cinnamon, nutmeg, salt, coconut oil, and vanilla.

3. Use clean, dry hands to combine all ingredients, working the mixture between your fingers until a crumbly texture forms. Divide in half, spreading one half in the prepared baking pan. Press firmly into the bottom of the pan to create an even crust.

4. Arrange the fresh blueberries in a single layer on top of the crust. Top with the remaining crumb mixture, breaking up large chunks and distributing evenly. Gently press to loosely pack the mixture.

5. Bake for 35 to 40 minutes, or until the top layer becomes golden brown and the blueberries start to bubble through the top layer. Remove from the oven and allow to cool for 5 to 10 minutes before serving.

SERVING SUGGESTION: Serve warm for a crumblier texture. If you prefer bars, allow to cool completely before cutting into 12 equal sections. Serve with additional fresh berries, your favorite yogurt, or vanilla ice cream.

PER SERVING:

Calories: 300; Total Fat: 18g; Saturated Fat: 12g; Polyunsaturated Fat: 3g; Monounsaturated Fat: 1.5g; Cholesterol: 0mg; Sodium: 100mg; Carbohydrates: 33g; Fiber: 4g; Sugars: 14g; Added Sugars: 9g; Protein: 6g

GRILLED PEACHES WITH CARDAMOM WHIPPED CREAM

Serves 4

PREP TIME: 10 minutes / COOK TIME: 5 minutes

30 MINUTES GLUTEN-FREE VEGETARIAN

Peaches are one of the few fruits I truly crave, and I genuinely miss them when they go out of season. During their fleeting time to shine, I stock up and enjoy them as often as I can. Grilling them is a fun way to work them into dessert instead of relying on them only for breakfast and snacks.

½ cup heavy (whipping) cream

1 tablespoon brown sugar

½ teaspoon vanilla extract

¼ teaspoon ground cardamom

4 ripe peaches, halved and pitted

1 tablespoon canola or grapeseed oil

1½ tablespoons honey, for drizzling

1. Use a hand or stand mixer to whip the heavy cream. Add the sugar, vanilla, and cardamom, and beat on high speed until peaks form. Chill in the refrigerator until needed.

2. Heat your grill or stove-top grill pan to medium heat. Brush the peach halves with oil to prevent sticking, then place flat-side down to sear. Grill for 4 minutes, or until grill marks form, then remove and place two halves in each serving bowl. Drizzle with the honey.

3. Remove the whipped cream from the fridge and divide evenly among the bowls. Serve immediately.

VARIATION: For a subtle change in flavors, try maple syrup or balsamic glaze instead of honey. You can also use vanilla Greek yogurt or kefir instead of the whipped cream for an added probiotic benefit.

PER SERVING:

Calories: 230; Total Fat: 15g; Saturated Fat: 7g; Polyunsaturated Fat: 1.5g; Monounsaturated Fat: 6g; Cholesterol: 40mg; Sodium: 15mg; Carbohydrates: 25g; Fiber: 2g; Sugars: 23g; Added Sugars: 10g; Protein: 2g

EASY MANGO SORBET

Serves 4

PREP TIME: 10 minutes, plus 2 to 4 hours to freeze

QUICK PREP GLUTEN-FREE VEGETARIAN

When I heard the word "sorbet," I always thought of something decadent and upscale. I didn't realize how simple it was to prepare at home with just a handful of ingredients. This easy recipe can be made with other types of fruit, but frozen mango is something I always keep stocked in my freezer.

½ cup coconut milk

½ cup sugar

1 (12-ounce) bag frozen mango chunks

1 tablespoon freshly squeezed lime juice

Fresh mint or basil, for garnish (optional)

1. In a small saucepan over low heat, make a syrup by heating the coconut milk. Add the sugar and let it dissolve completely, stirring often, about 2 minutes.

2. Add the syrup to a blender along with the frozen mango and lime juice. Blend until smooth, then transfer to a loaf pan or baking dish. Cover and place in the freezer for 2 to 4 hours, or until ready to serve. With an ice cream scoop or tablespoon, scoop out the sorbet into four small bowls. Top with the mint or basil before serving, if desired.

SERVING SUGGESTION: If using fresh herbs, chop or chiffonade (see tip, page 64) before serving. Sprinkle on cardamom or other favorite spices, if desired.

PER SERVING:

Calories: 210; Total Fat: 6g; Saturated Fat: 5g; Polyunsaturated Fat: 0g; Monounsaturated Fat: 0g; Cholesterol: 0mg; Sodium: 0mg; Carbohydrates: 39g; Fiber: 2g; Sugars: 37g; Added Sugars: 25g; Protein: 1g

LAYERED KEY LIME CUPS

Serves 4

PREP TIME: 10 minutes

QUICK PREP GLUTEN-FREE VEGETARIAN

Trust me when I say I'm no baker extraordinaire when it comes to desserts. I prefer to find inspiration in the desserts I love most and deconstruct them at home to make a simpler recipe. This is one example you'll see like that, where I've taken key lime pie and broken it down into an easy, layered dessert that takes only a short amount of time to prepare.

2 avocados, peeled and pitted

1 very ripe banana, peeled

¼ cup freshly squeezed key lime juice

1 tablespoon key lime zest, plus more for garnish

¼ cup maple syrup

1 teaspoon vanilla extract

2 pinches salt, divided

¼ cup Medjool dates, pitted and softened in warm water

¼ cup macadamia nuts, finely chopped, plus more for garnish

½ cup unsweetened coconut flakes

1 container (5.3-ounce) vanilla, low-fat Greek yogurt

1. In a blender, combine the avocado with the banana, key lime juice, key lime zest, maple syrup, vanilla, and 1 pinch of salt. Blend until a smooth, creamy texture forms.

2. Remove the dates from the water and pat dry. Add to the bowl of a food processor along with the macadamia nuts, coconut flakes, and the remaining pinch of salt for the crust. Process until a crumbly mixture forms.

3. Prepare four single-serving ramekins or low tumblers. Add the crust mixture to the bottom of each and gently pack down. Divide the avocado mixture evenly among them, then top each with a dollop of vanilla yogurt. Garnish with additional nuts or lime zest, if desired, and serve.

SUBSTITUTION: Macadamia nuts can be expensive, so if you prefer to substitute another type of nut, I recommend walnuts or pecans.

PER SERVING:

Calories: 390; Total Fat: 22g; Saturated Fat: 6g; Polyunsaturated Fat: 1.5g; Monounsaturated Fat: 12g; Cholesterol: 0mg; Sodium: 210mg; Carbohydrates: 49g; Fiber: 8g; Sugars: 37g; Added Sugars: 20g; Protein: 5g

CARROT CAKE COOKIES WITH TOASTED PECANS

Makes 18 cookies

PREP TIME: 10 minutes / COOK TIME: 15 minutes

30 MINUTES VEGETARIAN

My mother's favorite dessert is carrot cake, but baking is not one of my strengths. This recipe was inspired by the classic dessert but is much simpler to prepare, so I can make these treats for her on a whim.

Nonstick cooking spray
½ cup butter, softened
¾ cup granulated sugar
¾ cup tightly packed brown sugar
1 large egg
½ teaspoon vanilla extract
¾ cup all-purpose flour
¾ cup whole-wheat flour
1 teaspoon ground cinnamon
½ teaspoon baking soda
½ teaspoon baking powder
¼ teaspoon salt
1 cup shredded carrots
1 cup chopped pecans, toasted
½ cup raisins

1. Preheat the oven to 375°F. Prepare a baking sheet with nonstick cooking spray or parchment paper.

2. In a large bowl, cream the butter, granulated sugar, and brown sugar together until fluffy. Add the egg and vanilla, and stir to combine.

3. In another large bowl, combine the all-purpose flour, whole-wheat flour, cinnamon, baking soda, baking powder, salt, carrots, pecans, and raisins, then add to the wet ingredients. Fold together to form a thick batter.

4. Spoon the batter onto the prepared baking sheet, leaving about 1½ inches between each. Use a second baking sheet if needed. Bake for 12 to 14 minutes, or until the cookies are golden brown. Serve when they are cool enough, if you can wait that long.

SERVING SUGGESTION: Top each cookie with a dollop of cream cheese frosting and sprinkle with additional pecans (not included in nutritional analysis).

INGREDIENT TIP: If you're wondering whether both baking powder and baking soda are needed, the answer is yes. They are both leavening agents but add slightly different characteristics to the finished cookie. For best results, use the correct measurements of each.

PER SERVING (1 COOKIE):

Calories: 190; Total Fat: 10g; Saturated Fat: 3.5g; Polyunsaturated Fat: 1.5g; Monounsaturated Fat: 4g; Cholesterol: 25mg; Sodium: 120mg; Carbohydrates: 24g; Fiber: 2g; Sugars: 15g; Added Sugars: 8g; Protein: 2g

STONE FRUIT FOIL PACKETS WITH VANILLA ICE CREAM

Serves 4

PREP TIME: 10 minutes / COOK TIME: 10 minutes

`30 MINUTES` `VEGETARIAN`

Foil packet recipes are for more than just campfire meals! I love them because they eliminate virtually all cleanup so you can get down to enjoying this dessert without worrying about the mess. Whether you use the oven, grill, or an actual campfire, be sure to seal the foil packs so the fruit steams during cooking.

Nonstick cooking spray

2 large nectarines, halved and pitted

4 plums, halved and pitted

2 tablespoons loosely packed brown sugar

1 tablespoon lemon zest

Dash ground cinnamon

12 Nilla Wafers, crushed

3 cups vanilla ice cream (¾ cup per serving)

1. Preheat the oven to 350°F if not using a grill.

2. Prepare four foil packs by stacking two layers of aluminum foil, leaving plenty of room to fold and seal around the contents.

3. Lightly coat with nonstick cooking spray, then arrange one nectarine half and two plum halves in the center of each. Sprinkle one-quarter of the brown sugar, lemon zest, and cinnamon over each, then fold the edges of the foil up and over the contents, folding and pinching the edges to seal.

4. Place on the grill over medium heat or bake for 10 minutes. Remove from the heat and carefully vent the foil packs, taking care to keep fingers and faces away from the released steam.

5. Top the contents of each foil pack with the crushed wafers and vanilla ice cream and serve immediately.

VARIATION: Substitute peaches or cherries for alternative stone fruits. If not in season, pears, apples, or bananas can also be prepared this way. Granola or crushed shortbread cookies can be used in place of wafer cookies.

PER SERVING:

Calories: 350; Total Fat: 14g; Saturated Fat: 7g; Polyunsaturated Fat: 1g; Monounsaturated Fat: 3.5g; Cholesterol: 45mg; Sodium: 125mg; Carbohydrates: 53g; Fiber: 3g; Sugars: 44g; Added Sugars: 25g; Protein: 5g

LEMON CURD & RASPBERRY S'MORES

Serves 4

PREP TIME: 5 minutes / COOK TIME: 5 minutes

QUICK PREP VEGETARIAN

As much as I love chocolate, it doesn't pair with seafood quite the same way that fruity, citrusy flavors do. This version of the classic s'more can be made indoors just as easily as it can over a campfire. Use the Homemade Lemon Curd recipe (page 147) for a DIY version or swap in a premade or store-bought curd to speed up the process.

4 graham crackers

2 tablespoons Homemade Lemon Curd (page 147)

2 tablespoons raspberry jam or jelly

4 white chocolate squares

4 jumbo marshmallows

1. To make each s'more, break a graham cracker in half to form two squares. Spread the lemon curd onto one half and the raspberry jam or jelly on the other half. Place the white chocolate square on one half.

2. Toast the marshmallows over a grill, campfire, or stove-top burner. Once heated, place on top of the white chocolate square and top the s'more with the other half of the graham cracker. Serve immediately.

SERVING SUGGESTION: Mix up the fruits by swapping the raspberry jam for another variety.

PER SERVING:

Calories: 310; Total Fat: 8.5g; Saturated Fat: 4.5g; Polyunsaturated Fat: 0g; Monounsaturated Fat: 3g; Cholesterol: 50mg; Sodium: 215mg; Carbohydrates: 56g; Fiber: 0g; Sugars: 38g; Added Sugars: 26g; Protein: 3g

HOMEMADE LEMON CURD

Serves 8

PREP TIME: 10 minutes / COOK TIME: 5 minutes, plus 2 hours to chill

GLUTEN-FREE VEGETARIAN

If you prefer the DIY route, this simple lemon curd is surprisingly easy to make. This recipe will yield about 1 cup of finished lemon curd, so use leftovers for a topping in oatmeal, on muffins, or paired with other desserts or snacks.

1 large egg

3 large egg yolks

½ cup sugar

⅓ cup freshly squeezed lemon juice

2 tablespoons unsalted butter

Pinch salt

1½ tablespoons heavy (whipping) cream

1. In a small saucepan, whisk the egg, egg yolks, and sugar together. Once combined, turn the burner to low heat and whisk in the lemon juice, butter, and salt.

2. Slowly heat until the butter melts and the mixture starts to thicken. Heat to 170°F (about 5 minutes), and verify using a kitchen thermometer. Remove from the heat, stir in the cream, and transfer to a mason jar. Cover and chill for at least 2 hours before serving to allow the curd to set.

VARIATION: Once you've mastered this recipe, you can repeat it with other fruits. Try using the juice from pineapples, limes, pomegranates, or other fruits for a different flavor.

PER SERVING (2 TABLESPOONS):

Calories: 160; Total Fat: 6g; Saturated Fat: 3.5g; Polyunsaturated Fat: 0.5g; Monounsaturated Fat: 2g; Cholesterol: 105mg; Sodium: 55mg; Carbohydrates: 26g; Fiber: 0g; Sugars: 25g; Added Sugars: 25g; Protein: 2g

CHIPOTLE-CHOCOLATE CHIA PUDDING

Serves 2

PREP TIME: 5 minutes, plus 1 hour to chill

QUICK PREP GLUTEN-FREE VEGETARIAN

Chia puddings may be an acquired taste, but more so because of the texture. Chia seeds are easily flavored by other ingredients, but if you prefer a smoother texture, this blended recipe is for you. The spice keeps the flavor interesting and offers a unique contrast for a dessert that is traditionally very sweet.

½ cup chia seeds

1 cup 2% chocolate milk

1 teaspoon cocoa powder, unsweetened

½ teaspoon ground cinnamon

½ teaspoon vanilla extract

¼ teaspoon ground nutmeg

Pinch chipotle chili powder

½ tablespoon maple syrup or honey

Pinch salt

1. In a small bowl, cover the chia seeds with chocolate milk. Stir, then cover and refrigerate for at least 1 hour.

2. Remove from the refrigerator and transfer to a blender. Add the cocoa powder, cinnamon, vanilla, nutmeg, chili powder, maple syrup, and salt, and blend on high speed until a smooth texture forms. Use a spatula to scrape down the walls of the blender as needed.

3. Spoon into two bowls, and serve or store in the refrigerator for up to 3 days.

SERVING SUGGESTION: If you prefer it crunchy, garnish your pudding with mini chocolate chips, cacao nibs, or your favorite chopped nut (not included in nutritional analysis).

PER SERVING:

Calories: 350; Total Fat: 17g; Saturated Fat: 3g; Polyunsaturated Fat: 11.5g; Monounsaturated Fat: 2g; Cholesterol: 10mg; Sodium: 170mg; Carbohydrates: 41g; Fiber: 18g; Sugars: 18g; Added Sugars: 13g; Protein: 12g

BLANK SHOPPING LIST

VEGETABLES

BEANS/LEGUMES

FRUIT

NUTS/SEEDS

WHOLE GRAINS

OTHER

BLANK MEAL PLANNER

	SUNDAY	MONDAY	TUESDAY
Breakfast			
Lunch			
Dinner			

WEDNESDAY	THURSDAY	FRIDAY	SATURDAY

MEASUREMENT CONVERSIONS

OVEN TEMPERATURES

FAHRENHEIT (F)	CELSIUS (C) (approximate)
250°F	120°C
300°F	150°C
325°F	165°C
350°F	180°C
375°F	190°C
400°F	200°C
425°F	220°C
450°F	230°C

VOLUME EQUIVALENTS (LIQUID)

US STANDARD	US STANDARD (ounces)	METRIC (approximate)
2 tablespoons	1 fl. oz.	30 mL
¼ cup	2 fl. oz.	60 mL
½ cup	4 fl. oz.	120 mL
1 cup	8 fl. oz.	240 mL
1½ cups	12 fl. oz.	355 mL
2 cups or 1 pint	16 fl. oz.	475 mL
4 cups or 1 quart	32 fl. oz.	1 L
1 gallon	128 fl. oz.	4 L

WEIGHT EQUIVALENTS

US STANDARD	METRIC (approximate)
½ ounce	15 g
1 ounce	30 g
2 ounces	60 g
4 ounces	115 g
8 ounces	225 g
12 ounces	340 g
16 ounces or 1 pound	455 g

VOLUME EQUIVALENTS (DRY)

US STANDARD	METRIC (approximate)
⅛ teaspoon	0.5 mL
¼ teaspoon	1 mL
½ teaspoon	2 mL
¾ teaspoon	4 mL
1 teaspoon	5 mL
1 tablespoon	15 mL
¼ cup	59 mL
⅓ cup	79 mL
½ cup	118 mL
⅔ cup	156 mL
¾ cup	177 mL
1 cup	235 mL
2 cups or 1 pint	475 mL
3 cups	700 mL
4 cups or 1 quart	1 L

RESOURCES

America's Test Kitchen (americastestkitchen.com): A website featuring reviews of kitchen equipment and appliances, videos for culinary skills and techniques, and taste tests for ingredient comparisons, all intended for the home cook.

Best Food Facts (bestfoodfacts.org): Online resource through the Center for Food Integrity, providing evidence-based, expert answers to questions related to food, nutrition, and health topics.

***The Flavor Bible* and *The Vegetarian Flavor Bible* (karenandandrew.com):** Encyclopedia-style books to guide flavor pairings and ingredient combinations, listed alphabetically by ingredient.

Global Organization for EPA and DHA Omega 3s (goedomega3.com): A nonprofit trade association sharing research and information on EPA and DHA omega-3 fatty acids for consumers and health professionals.

National Fisheries Institute (aboutseafood.com): A nonprofit organization dedicated to education on seafood topics such as sustainability, health and pregnancy, nutrition, trade and commerce, and consumer protection.

NOAA FishWatch (fishwatch.gov): An online directory and resource to check the status of seafood species available in the United States and learn about sustainability for farmed and wild-caught fish.

Seafood Nutrition Partnership (seafoodnutrition.org): A nonprofit organization providing education to build the awareness and skills needed to improve diet quality through the consumption of seafood.

Seafood Watch® (seafoodwatch.org): Official program of the Monterey Bay Aquarium, providing resources and education to inform choices for farmed and wild-caught seafood. Includes a mobile app for convenient access while shopping.

SeaShare (seashare.org): A US-based nonprofit organization working to provide seafood for food banks and underserved families and promote sustainable practices in the seafood industry.

I also encourage you to check out my website, *Street Smart Nutrition* (streetsmartnutrition .com), dedicated to fearlessly nourishing meals. I share recipes similar to those featured here, as well as blog posts and resources for intuitive eating, sports nutrition, and a non-diet approach for health and well-being.

REFERENCES

Drouin-Chartier, Jean-Philippe, Julie Anne Côté, Marie-Ève Labonté, Didier Brassard, Maude Tessier-Grenier, Sophie Desroches, Patrick Couture, and Benoît Lamarche. "Comprehensive Review of the Impact of Dairy Foods and Dairy Fat on Cardiometabolic Risk." *Advances in Nutrition* vol. 7, no. 6, pp. 1041–105. Accessed August 1, 2018. https://www.ncbi.nlm.nih.gov/pmc/articles/PMC5105034/#!po=1.25000

Gil, Angel, and Fernando Gil. "Fish, a Mediterranean Source of *n*-3 PUFA: Benefits Do Not Justify Limiting Consumption." *British Journal of Nutrition*. Accessed August 1, 2018. https://www.cambridge.org/core/services/aop-cambridge-core/content/view/6B9F43B61A42E6EF5F5BA043500CFCCB/S0007114514003742a.pdf/fish_a_mediterranean_source_of_n3_pufa_benefits_do_not_justify_limiting_consumption.pdf

Hirahatake, Kristin M., Joanne Slavin, Kevin C. Maki, and Sean H. Adams. "Associations Between Dairy Foods, Diabetes, and Metabolic Health: Potential Mechanisms and Future Directions." *Metabolism*. Accessed August 1, 2018. https://www.ncbi.nlm.nih.gov/pmc/articles/PMC5367265/

Journal of the Academy of Nutrition and Dietetics. "Position of the Academy of Nutrition and Dietetics: Dietary Fatty Acids for Healthy Adults." Accessed August 1, 2018. https://jandonline.org/article/S2212-2672(13)01672-9/pdf

Lund, Elizabeth K. "Health Benefits of Seafood; Is It Just the Fatty Acids?" *Food Chemistry*, vol. 140, no. 3, 1 October 2013, pp. 413–420. Accessed August 1, 2018. https://www.sciencedirect.com/science/article/pii/S0308814613000575?via%3Dihub

The Nutrition Society. "The Future for Long Chain *n*-3 PUFA in the Prevention of Coronary Heart Disease: Do We Need to Target Non-Fish-Eaters?" *Proceedings of the Nutrition Society* (2017), 76, 408–418. Accessed August 1, 2018. https://www.cambridge.org/core/services/aop-cambridge-core/content/view/86D27F99040B2A44D13695E0A609142C/S0029665117000428a.pdf/future_for_long_chain_n3_pufa_in_the_prevention_of_coronary_heart_disease_do_we_need_to_target_nonfisheaters.pdf

RECICPE INDEX

INDEX

ABOUT THE AUTHOR

Cara Harbstreet, MS, RD, LD, is a Kansas City–based Intuitive Eating Registered Dietitian and nationally recognized food and nutrition expert. She obtained a Bachelor of Science degree in Dietetics and Nutrition from Southeast Missouri State University. She went on to complete her Dietetic Internship and Master of Science in Dietetics and Nutrition at The University of Kansas Medical Center. Upon completion, Cara worked in community nutrition, corporate wellness, retail, and outpatient clinical settings. In 2016, Cara founded her private practice and began focusing on sports nutrition, intuitive eating, and applying the Health At Every Size® (HAES) model for clients in the Kansas City area. Since then, she has expanded into virtual and telehealth services and serves as a consultant and nutrition communications expert. Cara is also an active volunteer in the dietetics field, serving as a multiyear Board Member for the Kansas Academy of Nutrition and Dietetics and the Sports, Cardiovascular, and Wellness Nutrition (SCAN) Dietetic Practice Group. She currently resides in Kansas City with her husband, dog, and two cats, all of whom enjoy the benefits of her culinary adventures in the kitchen.

CPSIA information can be obtained
at www.ICGtesting.com
Printed in the USA
BVHW061404231218
536277BV00020B/329/P

9 781641 522663